LAW AND CUSTOM IN BURMA AND THE BURMESE FAMILY

LAW AND CUSTOM IN BURMA AND THE BURMESE FAMILY

by

MAUNG MAUNG

B.L. (RANGOON), J.S.D. (YALE), LL. D. (UTRECHT),
OF LINCOLN'S INN, BARRISTER-AT-LAW

THE HAGUE
MARTINUS NIJHOFF
1963

ISBN 978-94-011-8518-9 ISBN 978-94-011-9257-6 (eBook)
DOI 10.1007/978-94-011-9257-6

PREFACE

This book, conceived in Rangoon, nourished and delivered at the Yale Law School, attempts to study the customary laws of Burma in the context of the country's legal system. Customary laws govern the affairs of the family mainly while codes and precedents designed and developed on the imported British common law system enjoy exclusive control and authority over the remaining legal relationships in society. This volume looks at the legal system in outline and the customary law of the Burmese family in some detail. The customary laws of other indigenous groups, such as the Shans, the Kachins, the Chins, the Kayah, the Mon and the Arakanese, also need to be studied, restated and appraised, for though the laws are similar there are shades of differences, and in building the Union of Burma it is important to build strongly on the similarities while giving due respect to the differences. It is, therefore, hoped, that this volume will launch a series of studies on the customary laws of the peoples of Burma in a large context and with high aim.

There are many needs for continuing research in the field of customary law. One is to discover the customs of the people as they really are, not just what they are presumed to be in early legal treatises or in later judicial decisions. Customs live and grow while treatises lag and become obsolete, and judicial decisions rendered by judges who have been trained in different schools of legal philosophy may go wrong."Before the transfer of power," said Dr. E. Maung, Supreme Court Justice, emphasising this need soon after Burma regained her independence in 1948, "the final court of appeal was the Privy Council in England. The Privy Councillors, though lawyers of great eminence, had not been trained in our peculiar system of law. Moreover the original texts were not available to them. The result was that the Privy Council, having before it only the Manugye and the Kinwunmingyi Digest in translation, had been led to make serious mistakes, with results which to the Burmese conscience appear shocking... Now that the Supreme Court is the final court of appeal and with judges who have access to the original texts and who can appreciate the conditions of the country and its social life, measures must be taken at the bar to rectify the mistakes made by the

Privy Council. To do that it is necessary that members of the Bar should study and understand the underlying principles of Burmese customary law and undertake a serious research of the development of legal notions in the system."[1]

Another need arises from Burma's new status of independence. Previously, the codes and the precedents supplied most of the country's legal needs. The codes were drafted on British common law principles adapted to local circumstances and needs; decisions of the High Court in England were of more than persuasive authority, and the opinions rendered by the Privy Council on appeals preferred from the decisions of the High Court of Judicature at Rangoon were of binding force. Thus, Burma's legal system moved in the full stream of the common law. Today there is a need and a desire to follow an independent course. "Now that our fate is in our own hands," said Justice E. Maung in his address referred to above," it is desirable that the development of our legal system should not slavishly follow the pattern set by the West. We should develop on our own lines and in conformity with our own native genius. A careful study of the early decisions and the history of administration of justice under the Burmese kings would be of the greatest help in this behalf. We who have been trained under the British common law system are apt to belittle our own native system, but a careful and comparative study of our laws will show that period for period, age for age, the Burmese jurists have not been lagging behind."

The opinions of the Privy Council no longer lay down binding precedents; they are "rules of wisdom" to which the Supreme Court may look for "guidance" in cases of need.[2] Nor would the Supreme Court of Burma, the court of final appeal, restrict itself in its search for guiding principles to the High Court in England and the Privy Council; a wider search and a deeper look into systems of common kinship but independent vigorous growth-- that of the United States, for example, of Canada, of Australia, and of India --have become a practice. Search and study can be beneficial, and borrowing, wisely done, can enrich. Yet, in shaping and building the legal system that will live and endure, care must constantly be given to make the system native, not alien, and towards that end, to bring it close to the hearts and the minds of

[1] Address to students of the law faculty, University of Rangoon, of whom the author was one, on the "Need for Research in Burmese Customary Law," reproduced in gist in the *Burmese Review*, Rangoon, December 13, 1949.

[2] Thus, for example, in *U Saw & 4 Others vs. The Union of Burma*, 1948 BLR 249. the Supreme Court adopted the tests used by the Privy Council in considering the admission of appeals in criminal matters.

the people. "The task facing the legislator - any legislator," writes Justice Moshe Silberg of the Supreme Court of Israel, where, as in Burma, tradition and modern institutions are learning to grow up together, "is to bring law closer to the mind (so that the people should understand it), and closer to the heart (so that they should want to obey it). If one of the two is lacking, a surrender to the law is perhaps possible, but not its observance."[1]

The call for drastic and wholesale revision has often been heard in Burma since independence. The popular cry, fortunately more often heard than heeded, is that the system inherited from the British was imposed by a colonial power and therefore tainted with tyranny. Such cries are heard often in Parliament when Opposition parties complain of "repressive laws" which give the Government the power to order "preventive detention" if it considers that public safety demands it.[2] The cry is also raised when the press claims freedom of expression in full, unfettered by registration requirements and laws which grant the Government emergency powers of search and seizure, or prescribe special penalties for the publication of "official secrets".[3] These cries, however, have been in the nature of protests against specific statutes which are found irkesome from time to time by some groups of the community. Calm and coordinated research and study has yet to be directed towards a reappraisal of the role of law in the community and the development of a legal system which represents a happy blend between tradition and progress. A law revision committee, appointed by the Government in 1951, wrestles with the task of tidying up the statute book and keeping up with the latest amendments; the primary task of revision remains virtually untouched despite the committee's valiant efforts to come round to it. Special *ad hoc* committees are appointed, as and when the clamour rises, to study the "repressive" and "undemocratic" laws and recommend their amendment or repeal. Much of what has so far been accomplished leaves an impression of a hurried patchwork. It is not that law-makers are unaware of the need for deeper

[1] Moshe Silberg: "Law and Moral in Jewish Jurisprudence," *Harvard Law Review*. December, 1961.

[2] E.g. debate on the question of law revision in the Chamber of Deputies, September 21, 1955, vol. 8, number 22 of the *Proceedings*, in Burmese, pp. 1475–1489.

[3] On November 13, 1961, newspapers carried on their front pages a "report to the people, in whom sovereignty resides," in which attention is drawn to "arbitrary laws, ordinances and emergency powers," and their being prone to abuse. "Colonial Laws" such as The Press Registration Act, 1867, The Press Emergency Powers Act, 1931, The Official Secrets Act, 1923, and The Printers and Publishers Act, 1959, were objected to. The Prime Minister and the Minister for Justice promised early legislation to remove repressive elements from press laws.

study and thinking and co-ordinated effort at all levels to build a system on a strong and broad base. Yet, the stresses and strains of nation-building in modern times often seem to set scales of priority in which creative law-making languishes somewhere near the bottom; or else, the Government, harassed and impatient, looks upon law as a weapon to wield rather than a tool to build with.

The search for the role of Buddhism in the State may also gradually turn thoughts towards introducing Buddhist ethics into law, giving due care to the preservation and protection of the principle of non-discrimination. Administered wisely and well the introduction may get those deep and widely shared beliefs and instincts of the people to add strength to the force of law. Administered too hastily or recklessly, it can cause damage and create new dangers. A similar situation seems to prevail in Israel where Professor Norman Bentwich, a former Attorney-General of Palestine, finds that while the British common law continues to exercise its influence "there is a movement, readily understandable, to introduce into the law of Israel elements from the Jewish system of law which goes back to the Bible, the Talmud compiled in the 5th. and 6th. centuries, and the rabinical codes of the Middle Ages. Jewish law may need to be modernised to fit present conditions; but it is likely to compete with the common law as a basis of fresh development... It helps, however, that the spirit of the common law is often the same as that of Hebrew law in the Bible."[1]

The customary law of the Burmese family, popularly and somewhat misleadingly called 'Burmese Buddhist Law', is secular in that it is not ecclesiastical law and the Buddhist religious order has no part to play in it, though it is not altogether free from the influence of Buddhist ethics. Thus, a study of the customary law can yield some clues as to whether, and if so how and to what extent, Buddhist ethics can be incorporated in the other areas of law.

This book, while turning its focus on the customary law of the Burmese family, will, it is hoped, bring into sharper relief the larger legal problems that stand in the wider context. It does not promise ready solutions to the problems, but it is hoped that it will make those problems a little clearer, and also emphasise the need for further research not in the 'legal' field only, but in the connected, often overlapping fields of study such as anthropology and the social sciences. Much of the materials for this study are drawn from legal sources, for

[1] *Law Quarterly Review*, Jan., 1960.

little has yet been done in the other fields, and it is hoped that Burmese and visiting scholars will, in happy and fruitful partnership, work to fill the gap in the years to come.

Perhaps visiting scholars will come from Yale University whose men have worked in far flung fields, and the Yale Law School whose teachers are now taking the torch of legal education into emergent Africa. The Yale Law School has been a stimulating, even a little intoxicating, experience for me these last two years. Here, it seems, to inform is a minor, almost unworthy, task for the teacher; his it is to excite and inspire, to fling down the challenge and have students rise up to it, to lead students on endless quests and expeditions; to incite irreverence for precedents and principles, however high they may come from, however old they may be. Here the spirit is that of challenge and crusade. In that spirit Dean Eugene Rostow of the School publicly congratulates his students who have been on 'freedom rides' in states where segregation laws linger somewhat shame-facedly; in that spirit Professor Fowler Harper marches through the United States Supreme Court and the courts of Connecticut at the vanguard of a battle to remove from the state's ancient statute book an obsolete law that renders some birth control practices illegal.[1] Here, the halls ring with the eloquence of Professor F. S. C. Northrop in his call to nations to dig hard to discover their 'living laws' and draw them forth and marshal them in the task of building the modern state; the meeting of East and West, the adventure of man, all these add up to the bright rainbow that Professor Northrop paints across the universe.[2] For Professors Myres S. McDougal, Harold Lasswell and associates also, the law lives and acts and plays in the active, unceasing social process in which man strives to achieve his goals through institutions and by the use of various resources. Man must have his values and his goals to render his life meaningful. Shared values and common goals can be forged as golden links to bind the community, or human communities across the globe, together. "Goal-thinking" is what the influential and expanding school of

[1] *Poe vs. Ullman*, 367 US 497, in which it was held that a suit seeking declaration of the unconstitutionality of a Connecticut statute barring the use of contraceptives did not present a justiciable controversy.

[2] "The major event of our time, as Professor Northrop of Yale University puts it," said U Nyo Mya, one of Burma's foremost writers, in a talk broadcast from Rangoon radio on the eve of the Festival of Lights, 1947, "is the meeting of East and West." He then went on to expound the good life as understood in Buddhism, and argue that the good life could be universal. *Burma Speaks*, a collection of broadcast talks, Government Information, Rangoon, 1950. *Philosophical Anthropology & Practical Politics*, by Professor F.S.C. Northrop, New York, 1960, is an important guide to this study.

Mc Dougal and Lasswell stresses. If man knows where he wants to go, he will soon invent the means of getting there.

To the faculty and staff of the Yale Law School I owe much for the help I received in the preparation of this book. The Graduate School and the Southeast Asia Studies Programme at Yale which received me on the faculty for two years, Dr. R. A. Holden, Professors Benda, Cornyn, Dahl and Pelzer, Miss Veronica O'Neal and Miss Ruth Borel were among those who made the two years' sojourn in New Haven pleasant and productive for my family and myself: among other things we produced three new books, one new edition, and one new baby who looks like the old editions.

There are many others, too numerous to fully list, who have inspired, helped and encouraged: Dean Myint of the law faculty, University of Rangoon, who gave life and beauty to Burmese customary law in his lectures which I attended some sixteen years ago; Professor Alan Gledhill, formerly a Judge of the High Court of Burma, now at the London School of Oriental Studies, Mr. G. R. Rajagopaul, Additional Secretary, Ministry of Justice, New Delhi, U Bo Gyi, Chief Judge of the new Chief Court of Burma, U Sin, my father, Higher Grade Pleader in Mandalay, U Htin Leong, Director of the Government Press, Rangoon, and U Ko, District and Sessions Judge, who supplied me with material and advice in our long-distance communications; my helpmate and friendly critic, Ma Khin Myint; many many friends.

New Haven,
Connecticut,
June, 1962.

MAUNG MAUNG

CONTENTS

CHAPTER ONE

BURMESE CUSTOMARY LAW

1. ORIGIN AND GROWTH

This present, Badda world began, in Burmese myth and legend, after previous worlds had been destroyed seven times by fire and once by water. This earth emerged as the water fell away, and a lotus flower blossomed to announce that on this earth a Buddha would appear.

The first living beings on this earth were the Byamhas whose terms in the celestial state had ended. These first inhabitants were good and pure. Happiness was their food, and the glow from their bodies lit the earth. Gradually, however, desire took them, and they ate the flavoured flakes of earth which were pleasant and mild and nourished their bodies without forming excrements. Greed only grew and they ate whatever that could find and grab; excrements formed, sexual organs developed, and lust came to the men and women, as they then became. They built houses in wich they could hide and hoard and live their lives of shame. Greed and lust led them to steal.

The men and the women at last decided that they must not let things decline further. They met in council and decided to elect a man from among them, a man of honesty, wisdom and worthiness, a man who would make the laws and instruct them, who would revile those who needed to be reviled, banish those who must be banished from the community. They sought and found the perfect one and crowned him their King, the Maha Thamada, and gave him power to rule and command, and a tenth of their flavoured rice. This King, he ruled wisely and well. He honoured those who were learned and good, and made a judge of a young cow-herd whose fame for wisdom had spread. Manu, this judge and minister, settled many disputes, and pronounced judgements of such wisdom that not men only but the Nats applauded.

Yet, Manu, whom the King had made noble, only wanted to lay down the burden of his office and the responsibility of judging his fellow men. In one dispute Manu gave a wrong decision. Two neighbours came to fighting over a cucumber fruit. The creeper grew in the garden of one and had spread into that of the other neighbour who plucked the fruit that the creeper bore on his side. The man in whose land the creeper had its roots claimed the fruit, but Manu, the wise one, decided that his claim must fail, and for once neither men nor Nats applauded the decision. Manu knew then that he had erred, and he thought again, and decided that the fruit came not from the creeper but from its roots and must belong to him in whose land the roots drew their nourishment, even as man in the present existence drew strength and destiny from his deeds in the past in the cycle of existences. So judged Manu, and men and Nats who heard him applauded.

But Manu, having erred, feared to err again, and begged his King for permission to go on a long quest for truth, and his own emancipation. The King sadly granted the permission and Manu went away to search and wander. Manu was able to gradually shake himself free from the shackles that bound him to the earth, and in lifting joy he ascended and on the "boundary wall of the solar system" he found laws engraved in "letters as large as elephants, horses, buffaloes or oxen," and these laws he copied and gave to the Maha Thamada to serve as the guide of wise and good men in their decisions. These, the Laws of Manu, were thus received and handed down through the generations as guide to Kings and men, and those that studied them and lived by them found happiness.[1]

This is a colourful tale, though not unsimilar to such tales told of the beginning of society and law in other lands. This tale is still told in Burma in varying versions in the books and the songs. The beginning of the earth is described in full colour in the songs, and the first blush of love among those earliest ancestors is something of which today's lovers sing with fondness, not shame. Yet, the tale is not all romantic imagination, for it has in it some living notions and beliefs. The notion of social contract whereby men joined to entrust the powers and responsibilities of leadership to a man is perpetuated today in parliamentary and representative institutions. The notion of command as the life and force of law is also there in the story, but the Maha Thamada himself was human, not a divine being, and he was not above the law. The discovery of the laws on the boundary wall of the solar system hints at divine revelation, but this was no more than the usual borrowing by man from some source above and beyond to give added strength and dignity to his laws. The notion of law as neither more nor less than a guide to wise and good decision, harmonious and happy living, still endures even under the increasing stresses and strains of the modern state. That

[1] D. Richardson, *Laws of Manu*, translation, Rangoon, 1896, pp. 4–18; Htin Aung, "Customary Law in Burma," in Burma 5th. anniversary number, Government Information, Rangoon, 1953.

notion, which reflects the nation's mind and heart, often fascinates and intrigues – sometimes exasperates – the visitor. "I do not think the Burman will ever make what we call a great nation," observed Fielding Hall, the British scholar and administrator who spent many years among the Burmese, "he will never try to be a conqueror of other peoples, either with the sword, with trade, or with religion. He will never care to have a great voice in the management of the world. He does not care to interfere with other people: he never believes interference can do other than harm to both sides. He will never be very rich, very powerful, very advanced in science, perhaps even in art, though I am not sure about that. It may be he will be very great in literature and art. But, however that may be, in his own idea his will always be the greatest nation in the world, because it is the happiest."[1]

As for renunciation, it is not Manu alone, but kings and ministers who have come after him, whose 'ambition' is to lay down the burden of office and seek peace for the soul. Aung San, architect of Burma's independence at the young age of 32, hoped that he might be able to relinquish office and devote himself to learning and educating his children.[2] U Nu, his successor, has always had as his highest ambition the life of a writer, to be, as he has often put it, "the Bernard Shaw of Burma," and that of a Buddhist lay missionary. "U Nu always wished to become a hermit," remembers Sir Hubert E. Rance, the British Governor who handed over power on January 4, 1948, "and to forsake public life. He came to power quite fortuitously. The majority of the Cabinet and General Aung San were assassinated on July 19,1947. U Nu was not in the Cabinet, but was one of the powers behind that political party, the Anti-Fascist People's Freedom League. After the assassination, I sent for him and asked him to form a new Government, which he did. But he told me in the months that followed, and we then knew that we were going to leave, that when I went he intended to go as well and to follow up this idea of his becoming a hermit, forsaking his family and children and going to a hilltop. With the greatest difficulty I persuaded him to stay saying that, 'I won't leave Burma until you make me a promise that you will stay for 6 months,' which promise I did get from him."[3] The situation in Burma did not permit U Nu to leave office entirely in the decade and half that followed the proclamation of independence, but the hope persisted, as was apparent in his

[1] H. Fielding Hall, *The Soul of a People*, London, 1904, p. 115.
[2] Maung Maung, *Aung San of Burma*, Martinus Nijhoff, 1962.
[3] H.E. Rance, "Burma Today" in *Asian Survey*, London, July, 1956.

statement to the press made in December, 1961. "As you know," U Nu said, "I will quit politics when the next general elections take place two years hence. I intend to go to India to propagate the Buddhist faith to the best of my ability. Buddhism is received by Burma from India, and laymen and monks alike should go to India to promote Buddhism by way of repaying our debt to India."[1]

All these, and others, that have happened in Burma's recent history – Aung San's plan to retire after he had helped to recover independence, U Nu's to leave after he had helped to consolidate it, or General Ne Win's eagerness to return to the command of the armed forces after handing over political power to the political parties at the end of a caretaker regime, 1958-60 – all these are parts in the continuum of Burmese life and law. In making modern laws also, the virtue of renunciation is often expounded to give persuasive force to the legislation, if not its entire meaning. Thus, in 1948, a few months after independence, in moving a bill in Parliament to provide for nationalization of agricultural land and its distribution among the peasants, Prime Minister U Nu emphasised the transient nature of property, and the wisdom of using it, therefore, only as means to a noble end. "Property," he said, "is meant not to be saved, not for gains, nor for comfort. It is to be used by men to meet their needs in respect of clothing, food, habitation, in their journey towards nirvana or heaven."[2]

Not in its philosophy only, but in its growth also, Burmese law has enjoyed continuity. "Its stream has not been stemmed or diverted by multiplicity of legislation; and a weight of legislative rules divorced from established principles had never been allowed to choke the life of principles. Burmese law in its descent to the latter part of the 19th. century had no breaks and catastrophes. Dynasties passed away to be succeeded by other dynasties; kings waged war with and supplanted other kings; rebellion on many occasions reared its head and pretenders had come to rule; but there never was a revolution in the growth of Burmese law."[3]

[2] *Burma Weekly*, Government Information, Rangoon, December 14, 1961.

[2] Land Nationalization, speeches made in Parliament, and the Bill, Government Information, Rangoon, 1948; also Maung Maung, *Burma's Constitution*, 2nd. ed., Nijhoff, 1962, p. 105 – the book is a study of the constitution and its history including the Ne Win caretaker government.

[3] E. Maung, *Expansion of Burmese Buddhist Law*, Rangoon, 1951.

2. HINDU INFLUENCE AND THE DHAMMATHATS

Manu, the law-giver, cow-herd or hermit, minister or judge, in whatever garb he appeared, came with the tide of Hindu learning and civilization. "When the Pilgrim Fathers left the shores of Europe to found a new world in the West, they took with them their supreme code of law, the Bible. In like manner, a thousand or more years earlier, the emigrants from India, Hindu and Buddhist, who laid the foundations of a new world in the Tropical Far East, took with them their law book, the Code of Manu. Everywhere throughout the region Manu has left his mark: in Burma both among Mon and Burman, in Siam, Cambodia, Java and Bali. To follow him through his various incarnations, Hindu and Buddhist, in these various countries would be a fascinating problem, and should throw much light upon the course of Indian influence in Further Asia."[1]

Hindu learning, more than Hindu jurisprudence, influenced the growth of Burmese legal thought and literature, however. The Hindu Code of Manu was used more as a model for legal treatises than for its contents; the name of Manu was impressive and inspiring, and it was frequently invoked in the treatises that were written after the Code had been received. "So has Manu decided." But it was not Hindu law that the wise Manu expounded in the Burmese texts, it was Burmese law and custom, and Manu was the convenient and prestigious mouthpiece. By the time the Hindu influence – and stimulant was felt, Burmese society had become well organized in the village communities, in the small cities and the small kingdoms, and these communities had developed their cultures and customs, their laws and their government, and above all, a capacity to borrow and receive from other migrant civilizations without being overwhelmed. The spread of Buddhism – in revolt against the elaborations of Brahmanism – also offset the Hindu influence. Buddhism waxed with the ascent of Asoka to the throne of the Magadhan empire in 269 B.C., and under his care it rose to the stature of a world religion. Burma received Buddhism as it came over the sea routes to her coastal areas. An overland trade route also existed between India and China "from at least 128 B.C. by the north-east frontier and Burma. Buddhism spread thus into Yunnan, and intercourse was quickened from 69 A.D. when China advanced to the present fron-

[1] J.S. Furnivall, "Manu in Burma," *Journal of the Burma Research Society*, vol. xxx, pt. 2, August, 1940.

tier of Burma."[1] Buddhism had strong appeal for the communities in Burma which received it, and it flourished and attained pruity and lasting life. "In Burma, and in Burma alone throughout India, "wrote Sir Herbert Thirkell White, who was Judicial Commissioner of Upper Burma, and later Lieutenant-Governor of the Province when it was a part of the Indian Empire, "Buddhism is a vital force. The suggestion that religion is in danger, or that monks have been ill-used, is the surest way to rouse popular feeling. The ethics of Buddhism are as lofty and inspiring as those of any faith in the world. Obviously Burmans do not invariably shape their lives in strict accordance with the precepts of the law. But in spite of failings and shortcomings, the spiritual and moral force of their religion sheds a penetrating influence on national life and character."[2]

Burmese legal treatises came thus to invoke not Manu alone but the 'Three Gems,' the Buddha, the Law, and the Priesthood. A treatise would open with this kind of invocation: "May the Law which, having originated in the mouth of the Buddha, the Lord of rahans, is pure and excellent, and which is the refuge of all sentient beings, inspire me with pleasure."[3] Customary laws that were attributed to Manu, the law-giver, came to be attributed to Buddhist doctrines. "With the establishment of Buddhism and the spread of Buddhist doctrine," observed the Privy Council on an appeal from Burma, "came, in course of time, the not unnatural desire to strengthen the sanctions of juridical rule by associating its foundations, the Dhammathats themselves, with the religious sentiments of the people, and in the later Dhammathats, the commands, precepts, and principles are represented as truly being emanations from the spirit of Buddha himself."[4]

Hindu law dropped out of Burmese jurisprudence much in the same way as Roman law came to be forgotten in England. The names of the several forms of adoption can be traced to Hindu law; but the Burmese system has departed far from the prototype. The Brahman has no influence, though he is mentioned in the older books, but only in the form of an inaccurate summary of his peculiar ways. Ancestor worship is absent in the Burmese system; family names are unknown; inheritance does not depend on the capacity of the heirs to take part in offerings to the spirits of the deceased. There is no joint family as known to the

[1] Arthur Eggar, *Laws of India*, pt. I, London, 1929, p. 12, relying on the authority of Prof. G.H. Luce of the University of Rangoon.
[2] Sir Herbert Thirkell White, *A Civil Servant in Burma*, London, 1913, p. 192.
[3] *Kinwunmingyi Digest*, 2 vols., Rangoon, 1909.
[4] *Ma Hnin Bwin vs. U Shwe Gon*, 8 LBR 1.

Hindus, although the notion of ancestral property has remained in vague outline, and the heirs have a right of pre-emption so as to keep property in the family. The chief difference between the two systems is due to the Buddhist notion of the equality of the sexes which has resulted in marriage being a partnership in goods, vesting an equal interest in each spouse.[1] "When greater races bound the feet or veiled the face of their women," writes Mr. Harvey, the historian, "or doubted if she had a soul, the Burmese held her free and enthroned her as chieftainess and queen."[2] The equal status enjoyed by women is a feature that is shared by other countries of the region. Thus, in Burma and Siam, for example, "the doctrines of Buddhism have produced a striking, and to the lover of true civilization a most interesting result, *viz.* the almost complete equality of the conditions of women with those of men. In those countries, women are not miserably confined in the interior of their houses, without the remotest chance of ever appearing in public. They are seen circulating freely in the streets; they preside at the comptoirs, and hold an almost exclusive possession of the bazaars. Their social position is more elevated in every respect than that of the persons of their sex in the regions where Buddhism is not the predominating creed. They may be said to be men's companions and not their slaves. They are active, industrious and by their labours and exertions contribute their full share towards the maintenance of the family. The marital rights, however, are fully acknowledged by a respectful behaviour towards their lords."[3] The customary law of the family in Buddhist Southeast Asia is therefore, to a large extent, the common law of the region.

The Dhammathats, or treatises of "rules which are in accordance with custom and usage and which are referred to in the settlement of disputes relating to person and property," are a principal source of Burmese customary law.[4] They are not codes of law in the strict sense, and there is wide variance among them in content and quality. They reflect the social customs of the day, and expound rules of wisdom as guides for kings, ministers, and judges to rule by and for the people to live by. They record decisions, real or imaginary, to establish rules of persuasive force. They are, as Sangermano called the translations which he appended to his book, "The Golden Rules." Some of the recorded

[1] Eggar, *Laws of India*, pp. 14–15; Htin Aung, *Customary Law in Burma*.
[2] G.E. Harvey, *History of Burma*, London, 1925.
[3] Sangermano, *The Burmese Empire*, Rangoon, 1893, see introduction by Sir John Jardine.
[4] *Kinwunmingyi Digest*, I, p. 2.

decisions are haphazard collections which do not establish principle or precedent. Thus, for example, "the law of inheritance as set forth in the Dhammathats is not, strictly speaking, a system of law, but a congeries of decisions which are usually pronouncements *ad hoc* upon particular cases as they have arisen, and which for the most part do not purport to be determined persuant to any general or guiding principle."[1]

Some of the Dhammathats were described by Justice E. Maung as "cram books – though I had my colleagues on the Bench protesting vehemently – such is the ingrained reverence we have for the Dhammathats. Let me cite the Pakinnaka Dhammathat, written in 1835 A.D. by Zeya Pyanchi, as a case in point. The author, a Judge in the reign of King Bagyidaw, the seventh king of the Alaungpaya dynasty, recalled how he had played truant in his younger days and how, when he succeeded his father in his hereditary office, he repented the wasted years of his youth and late in life resumed his studies of the law. He then told us how for the benefit of his two sons Maung Thiha and Maung Eka, who he hoped would not follow in his earlier footsteps, he had prepared the metrical text for their study. An analogy may perhaps be found in Littleton on Tenures, written in 1475 A.D. – and on which Chief Justice Coke built his commentary – also for the benefit of and addressed to his son, then a student at Cambridge."[2]

The History of the Pitakas, compiled by the royal librarian under the last Kings of Mandalay, lists 175 treatises, of which the Dhammathats proper are 57, the Hpyat-hton or Rulings 82, the Compendia and Digests 10, and the Linka or Verses 26.[3] Professor E. Forchhamer, a great oriental scholar, marked three periods in the development of Dhammathat literature: the first ending with the break-up of Bayinnaung's empire in 1600 A.D., the second ending with the Talaing invasion of Ava in 1750 A.D., and the third covering the Alaungpaya dynasty, the last before Burma came under British rule. The last period was the most fruitful for "Alaungpaya and his successors again rallied prominent priests and laymen around them; they encouraged every branch of learning; Ava and Amarapura became the centres of religious life and learning of the Southern Buddhist Church; classical studies revived; the vernaculars were also culti-

[1] *Maung Thein Maung vs. Ma Kywe*, 13 Ran. 412 F.B.

[2] E. Maung, *Expansion of Burmese Buddhist Law.*

[3] Furnivall, *Manu in Burma*; E. Maung, J., in *Dr. Tha Mya vs. Daw Khin Pu*, 1951 BLR 108 S.C.

vated, and Burmese became the medium of philosophic and popular lore."[1]

Thirty-six Dhammathats were compiled and compared by Kinwunmingyi U Gaung for the Judicial Commissioner of Upper Burma when British rule was extended there, and the English translation of the Digest, published in two volumes, has become the most readily accessible repository of Burmese legal literature.[2] The authors, or compilers, of these Dhammathats were Buddhist monks, scholars, judges and ministers, and there was such difference between them in competence and intention that the first problem that presented itself to the British ruler was that of attaching correct weight to each Dhammathat. Sir John Jardine, Judicial Commissioner of British Burma, and a great scholar, thought, after much research, that Manugye was "fuller than most" though in his inquiries "among judges, advocates, and authors, I have been met with doubts; and I am convinced that a great part of the Manugye is generally ignored, while the Woonana Dhammathat has hardly been looked at..."[3] Manugye enjoyed the advantage of being written in Burmese prose, and the first translation in English was rendered by Dr. Richardson in 1847, and the Dhammathat became ready reference. For these reasons, and on the authority of Dr. Forchhammer, the Privy Council decided to give Manugye the pre-eminence among all Dhammathats, and that in disputed questions where Manugye provided clear answers other Dhammathats did not need to be consulted.[4] The myth of the pre-eminence of Manugye has, however, been finally shattered in a classic case in which the Supreme Court demonstrated that translations of it contained errors, and the Dhammathat itself had been confused in its borrowing from different sources.[5]

3. MIRRORS OF SOCIETY

The Dhammathats are useful, and used, as mirrors of the society of the day. They do not lay down the "law"; they reflect the customs and the rules which act and play in society, and when the reflections

[1] Jardine prize essay on *Sources and Development of Burmese Buddhist Law*, Rangoon, 1885.

[2] See appendix I for the 36 Dhammathats. Kinwunmingyi U Gaung served as chief minister to Thibaw, last King of Mandalay, and went on missions to Europe in last desperate efforts to win friends and alliances for Burma. He served as an adviser, when British rule came, and a member of the legislative council of the Lieutenant-Governor.

[3] *Notes on Buddhist Law*, Rangoon, circular memorandum number 31 of 1882.

[4] *Ma Hnin Bwin vs. U Shwe Gon.*

[5] *Dr. Tha Mya vs. Daw Khin Pu.*

are clear, the customs and rules are accepted as having binding force. Thus, "the Dhammathats are not the sole repository of Burmese customary law, which is also to be ascertained from decided cases and the prevailing customs and practices of Burma."[1] When the rules are uncertain, and there is no proof as to which Dhammathat ought to be followed, or what rule should prevail, when it cannot be shown which rule is the living law and which a dead letter, then the Courts accept a custom that is in consonance with equitable principles.[2]

The task of reconciling the customs as the Dhammathats record them, and those of changed society today, has presented Judges with problems as well as opportunity to make and mould the law. "The Court is not only at liberty but is bound to decide the case in accordance with Burmese customary law as it obtains today, rather than to perpetuate the outworn shiboleths of bygone ages... Burmans are not doomed to life forever under the rulings and customs by which they were governed in the days of King Alaungpaya."[3] The same spirit moved Dr. Ba U, the first Chief Justice of Burma after independence, to recall: "Some of the provisions of the Dhammathats are archaic and obsolete. They cannot be applied, therefore, in a wholesale fashion to the present state of society. They need to be trimmed or modified to suit modern Burmese life. Thus, where customary law has to be interpreted by non-Burmese judges, the help of the Burmese members of the bar is absolutely essential; otherwise the exposition can never be satisfactory, as it will not be in accord with the ideas and traditions of the Burmese people."[4]

To the modern student, even the division of the body of law into eighteen titles in the Dhammathats appears to be archaic. "Listen,O great King, attentively to the eighteen branches of law contained in this Dhammathat!" So exhorts Wagaru Dhammathat in article 2. "The law concerning the contracting of debt; the law of giving and taking (in marriage); the law of sale and purchase; the law regarding slaves; the law of inheritance; the law of gambling; the law of assault; the law of theft; the law regarding the hiring of persons; the law dealing

[1] Sir Arthur Page, C.J., in *Ma Hnin Zan vs. Ma Myaing*, 13 Ran. 487.

[2] *Ma Po vs. Ma Shwe Mi*, 2 UBR 79; Tha Gywe, *Treatise on Buddhist Law*, vol. I, Mandalay, 1909.

[3] *Ma Hnin Zan vs. Ma Myaing*; and compare Mr. Justice Holmes: "It is revolting to have no better reason for a rule of law than that it was laid down in the time of Henry IV. It is still more revolting if the grounds upon which it was laid down have vanished long since and the rule simply persists from blind imitation of the past." Ephraim London, ed., *The World of Law*, New York, 1960.

[4] Dr. Ba U, *My Burma*, New York, 1959, p. 112.

with adultery; the law of division of land; the law of purchase of property; the law relating to accusations; the law of deposit of property; the law of mortgage; the law of divorce; the law regarding two-footed and four-footed animals."[1] And the Manugye approvingly says: "These eighteen titles of law are settled as the groundwork of all judicial procedure in this word." A student of Austin's jurisprudence, complained a modern Burmese scholar, would be repulsed by the disorderly treatment; even the Twelve Tables of the Romans would be more scientific in their classification.[2] Some of the branches would seem to overlap, and some to deal with subjects that never did enjoy significant importance in Burmese society. Slavery was one of those subjects. Except for cases in the earlier days when debtors were required to serve off their obligations if they were unable to pay, or where Kings assigned groups of people by decree to the service of pagodas or the practice of lowly tasks, slavery as such was not an institution. In order, however, to finally extinguish slavery in all its forms, the framers of the constitution thought fit to write into it proper safeguards, and on the day the constitution came into life the President of Burma proclaimed: "As a consequence of royal mandates issued by previous rulers in our past history, there still exist in Burma persons who are obliged to be grave-diggers, beggars, pagoda slaves, monastery slaves, *thinkyis* and such like outcasts. I do hereby abrogate these royal mandates and permit such persons freely to enter into such trades and professions as they may choose out of their own free will and accord. As laid down in the constitution, let all citizens exercise and be accorded equal rights and privileges."[3]

The Dhammathats deal extensively, and freely, with the manners and morals of society, refusing to be confined to the province of pure law. Thus, for example, Dhammathats describe the "forty blandishments," or wiles of women, "so that all good men should know, and keep strict control over their wives and female attendants." The forty female wiles, which still seem to be practised universally with small variations and improvements, are: "1. stretching the body and arms, at sight of a man while standing near him, as a sign, whether pre-concerted or not, that he is thought of favourably by her and with a view of engaging

[1] *Wagaru Dhammathat*, English translation, Rangoon, 1892.
[2] Chan Toon, *Principles of Buddhist Law*, Rangoon, 1903, p. 20.
[3] Proclamation made by the President in Parliament, *Proceedings*, January 4, 1948, also in *Independence Celebration Number*, Government Information, Rangoon, 1948; chapter 2 of the constitution, defining fundamental rights: the Slavery Act, 1843, was an earlier legal measure against sale of persons, or compulsory labour or services.

affections; 2. letting something fall as if accidentally, and picking it up in such a manner as to show off her figure to the best advantage; 3. exhibiting studied elegance and gracefulness in dress and movements; 4. pretending to be modest by covering the exposed parts of her body or by leaning against a wall or screen; 5. scratching the nails of her hands and feet one against another; 6. trampling one foot by the other; 7. writing on the ground; 8. lifting up another's child or her own, or 9. making others lift him, 10. kissing him, or 11. making others kiss him, 12. playing with him, or 13. making others play with him, 14. embracing him, or 15. making others embrace him, 16. eating anything with him, or 17. making him eat something given by her, 18. giving him something such as flowers, fruits, etc. 19. asking from him the return of the thing given; 20. mimicking the child's movements; 21. speaking in praise or in disparagement of a man; 22. letting a man know her wishes in an overt, or 23. a covert manner, by signs such as dancing, singing, playing on musical instruments, weeping, moving about or dressing; 24. laughing boisterously to convey some secret meaning; 25. ogling at a man; 26. shaking the waist, 27. or some concealed part of the body; 28. exposing the thighs as if by accident, 29. pretending to cover them again; 30. exposing the breasts, 31. the armpit, 32. or the naval; 33. winking; 34. raising the eyebrows; 35. biting the lips; 36. protruding the tongue; 37. allowing her dress to slip off partly as if by accident; 38. re-arranging the dress, 39. loosening hair already tied in a knot, and 40. tying loose hair into a knot.[1] These wiles are not illegal, but they are for all good men to be wary of.

Other than the wiles, there are five improprieties that a woman may be guilty of: "with regard to food, when she takes her meals before her husband does so; or when she indulges often in her husband's absence in eating rich food; or when she gets up late in the morning and the first thing she does is eat; or when she eats stealthily the greater portion of any food obtained and leaves only a little of it for her husband; with regard to behaviour towards men when her conduct towards all men she comes across is as free as towards her husband; with regard to dress if she puts on inappropriate dresses when she attends feasts, or stays at home, or goes on a journey, or attends to her duties as a wife and as a mother; with regard to property when she gives away, sells, or mortgages it without the knowledge of her husband; and with regard to looking when she looks at a man with eyes as restless as those of a crow; or when she is in the habit of looking at men when they are dressing or

[1] *Kinwunmingyi Digest*, II, p. 20.

undressing, or when they are bathing."[1] A guilty wife may not be given brutal punishment, but shall be gently chastised, "by beating her on the back and the buttocks with a cane, split bamboo, or the palm of the hand."[2] These also, the improprieties as well as the punishments, have become obsolete with the passage of time and the changes that society has undergone.

Contract debts, and the King will pay, is also a maxim that has lost validity and only remains a pleasant myth and a pious hope in these days of increasing income-tax and other taxes. In the earlier days the King was exhorted to provide those citizens who needed assistance with capital, recoverable only after three years, and then in easy instalments and without interest. It was not all Kings who handed out such interest-free loans to needy subjects; history, in fact, has record of Kings who expected, and exacted, more than their "one-tenth share of flavoured rice" from their subjects. Yet, there was the moral duty, and "to Burmese jurists, almost all of whom received their education in religious institutions and not a few of whom were members of the Buddhist religious order, it was but a short step from such moral exhortations to legal obligations binding on the ruler."[3]

While obsolete rules are left to lie on the pages of treatises, written on palm leaves and preserved through time or collected in printed digests, those that truly reflect the deep beliefs and faiths, the constant manners and morals of Burmese society, have continued to live and grow in its daily doings, and come to be recognized as law in the decisions of the Courts. Judicial sanction and, perhaps more potently, popular disapprobation for the offenders, uphold the living customs, and as they are not cast in the rigid mould of statutes, they grow freely even as society grows. These Burmese customary laws are civil, not criminal, laws, and secular, not ecclesiastical laws. Buddhist ethics have doubtless influenced their development, but the term, "Burmese Buddhist Law," which was fixed on them under British rule and which has passed into common usage, is strictly a misnomer. "Buddhist means what appertains to the Buddhist faith," Maung Ba, J., pointed out, "and Buddhism has laid down no law which is to be applied to secular matters. We have, however, a number of law books entitled Dhammathats which are primarily intended to apply to Burmans. The religion of that race is Buddhism which was also the State religion when the Burmese monarch was on the

[1] *ibid.* p. 18.
[2] *ibid.*, p. 151.
[3] E. Maung, "Insolvency Jurisdiction in Early Burmese Law," *Journal of Burma Research Society*, December, 1951.

throne. So the Dhammathats intended for the Burmese Buddhists have come to be know as the Burmese Buddhist Law or the Buddhist Law."[1]

The Dhammathats have fallen behind as time moves on. Judicial decisions have culled out their essence in a large measure but decisions can only be rendered on questions that are brought to the Courts and they can give life and continuity to customs only to the extent that judges and lawyers are aware of them. Mirrors to fully and faithfully reflect these customs, these living laws that change almost imperceptibly as they flow in the stream of continuity, are much in need.

4. ADMINISTRATION OF JUSTICE

The main aim of Burmese traditional justice is to achieve harmony and peace in society. The judges and arbitrators are there primarily to give patient ear to the litigants and gently guide them to compromise. The procedures are neither formal nor rigid. In the village, the elders serve as mediators and arbitrators, and it is to them that villagers take their disputes or their family problems. Decisions are guided by considerations of what is good for the peace and harmony of the village or the family; often the decisions do not need to be handed down – they are arrived at as the disputants argue their angers out. Where guiding principles are needed the Dhammathats are referred to, or recalled, or tales from the Buddhist Jataka cited, or the wisdom of the Pyatton or Rulings drawn on.[2] The Pyatton or collections of decisions rendered by Princess Thudamasari, for example, are well read in Burmese literature even today, as are the decisions of Mahawthata, the wise prince and embryo Buddha. But these are not law reports as the lawyer today understands them. The system of mediation and arbitration has survived in the village, with some modifications, to the present day, and not in family problems only but in the general social problems of the village as well. Outside the village, however, the system has been subjected to drastic change as laws get modernised and the judicial hierarchy becomes more formal and organized.

[1] *Ma Yin Mya vs. Tan Yauk Pu*, 5 Ran. 406, F. B., at p. 421.

[2] U Nu and other leaders have used the Jataka tales with good effect to enforce or emphasise their points in parliamentary debates and public speeches. For judicial procedure in early Burmese days: E. Maung, *Expansion of Burmese Buddhist Law;* Maung Maung, *Burma in the Family of Nations*, Amsterdam, 1956, pp. 14–20; Shwe Yoe, *The Burman, His Life and Nations*, London, 1910, chap. 55; Than Tun, "The Legal System in Burma, 1000–1300 A. D.," *Burma Law Institute Journal*, Rangoon, June 1959.

"Sometimes the village judges who had done well were recognized by the King," recalled Taw Sein Kho, an eminent Burmese scholar, "and some of them were turned into appellate judges. They were not paid by the Government at all. They received a very small amount of fees from litigants, and the judges being permanent residents of the villages nothing unfair or unjust was done. They were actually arbitrators whose great idea was to settle all disputes on the principle of compromise."[1] Appellate judges were drawn from many quarters: learned men – or women – of modest circumstances might attract the attention of the King by their works of scholarship, and receive appointments as ministers or judges. There was no aristocracy or professional class to which selection was restricted. "The Burmese are a community of equals," observed Fielding Hall, "in a sense that has probably never been known elsewhere. All their institutions are the very opposite of feudalism. Now, feudalism was instituted to be useful in war. The Burmese customs were instituted that men should live in comfort and ease during peace: they were useless in war."[2]

Six classes of judges were recognized in the traditional form of Burmese justice. The parties themselves, if they could argue out their dispute and reach agreement, were recognized as the best judges in their own cause. Or they could appoint one or more arbitrators of their own. Then, there was the unpaid but officially appointed and recognized arbitrator, whose court was the Khon-Yon. Above this there was the court of the district officer. Then the chief civil court at the capital, and finally, the King – "the mighty fountainhead of justice," though he was not himself above the law – and the Hluttaw, Supreme Court and Privy Council combined. The heir apparent or a designated prince would preside over the judicial sessions of the Hluttaw whose recommendations the King would normally accept. Petition could, however, be laid with the King to review the Hluttaw's findings.

Proceedings in an elaborate suit would go like this. "The commencement of a suit is by the presentation of a written plaint, on which the Judge commonly orders an assistant called nakhan (listener) to enquire into the case and report. The nakhan examines the parties and perhaps their witnesses and presents his report. With this the parties submit their pleading, full statement of cause of action, and reply or defence.

[1] Burma Reforms Committee, *Record of Evidence*, vol II, Rangoon, 1922, p. 73.

[2] *The Soul of a People*, p. 54; for qualifications of a judge, see Rajaniti, para 10: "He shall be appointed a judge who is full of family piety and virtue, who maintains the true law, who is full of wisdom, amiable, and shrewd." J. Gray, *Ancient Proverbs and Maxims from Burmese Sources*, London, 1886.

A day is then appointed for hearing, advocates are chosen, and the case is heard. After the necessary examination of the parties and their witnesses, issues are fixed by the Judge, who at the same time declares on whom the burden of proof lies. Thus, the order runs: 'let the plaintiff prove so and so,' or 'let the defendant, if he can, prove so and so.' Witnesses are examined after this, and judgement is given. If the parties agree to abide by the judgement, they both eat tea, and the judgement thus becomes final. If they do not so agree, they may appeal to a higher grade of court. Sometimes, if the worsted party is considered unreasonable and contumacious, he is imprisoned for a time to compel him to 'eat tea' and accept the court's decision."[1] In the Hluttaw business was conducted with ceremonial and solemnity. The members of the court wore their robes and insignia; lawyers wore robes provided from the public purse and kept at the court, and the lawyer representing the plaintiff wore a green cap, and the lawyer representing the defendant a red; parties to the dispute also wore distinctive dress.

Lawyers were there, the chronicles and the treatises say, even in the 5th. century B.C., but that was perhaps too early. By about 12th. century A.D., however, the legal profession had, as evidenced by reliable records, established itself in the judicial system. Judges did not seem to have looked upon the advent of lawyers with great enthusiasm. Several royal edicts issued in the ensuing period appeared to have been aimed at curbing the activities of lawyers. Special dress was prescribed for them, including a conical head-dress, a bag holding a drinking cup hanging from the shoulder, a fan with a long yellow handle to hold in the hand; special quarters were allotted in the city for lawyers to live in, perhaps so that clients might readily find lawyers to engage, or that citizens might more safely avoid the long-winded class, perhaps both. It was recognized, however, that lawyers were necessary to better present the cases of the less articulate citizens, and for services rendered lawyers were permitted to collect one-tenth of the value of the subject of dispute, and later, thirty seven and three-eighth ticals of silver, and that even if they were not called upon by the court to answer the pleas of the opposite side. An edict of 1636 A.D. laid down the ethics and functions of

[1] Jardine, *Notes on Buddhist Law*, part, 2, p. 16; eating pickled tea, though no longer practised in the courts, is still referred to as symbolic of amicable settlement, e. g., Prime Minister U Nu to Justice Minister Dr. E. Maung on the subject of a running feud between the Government and the Press – "Don't say anything to them, just keep quiet. I take the appearance of such huge black banner-lines as presaging a good meal to be offered by journalists just as they made us relish the pickled tea when the previous feud ended." *Burma Weekly*, Government Information bulletin, Rangoon, December 7, 1961.

good lawyers; "to put the client's case to the best advantage before the court, in the light of their legal learning, and having due regard to the time and circumstances; to advise the client if he had a weak case, and if the client persisted, to seek to minimize the damage to the client." Lawyers who sought to pervert the ends of justice were, the edict added, no better than thiefs and robbers.[1] Bad lawyers inevitably, and even good lawyers sometimes, were expected to end up in hell, and the Burmese hell, as every child knows from the mural paintings on the ceilings of pagodas, is a very uncomfortable place.

Documentary evidence excluded oral testimony; when documents existed they must be put in and proved, and only in their absence could their contents be established by secondary oral evidence. Judges were enjoined to seek the substance of the case, unhampered by procedural formality, and give full and final justice so that vexatious litigation on the matter might end. Certain types of people were not accepted as witnesses: "great talkers, sick persons, old men, children, gluttons, gamblers, hot-tempered people, thieves, public singers, those who do not believe in the merit of good works, actresses, pregnant women, women of ill fame," being among those incompetent classes.[2] Exceptions came to be allowed in the rules of evidence. Those who were incompetent could be examined if the parties consented; female witnesses were preferred if they were trust-worthy, to male witnesses who did not appear to be so; an earlier rule requiring a certain minimum number of witnesses to establish a point was abrogated.

The exclusion of women as witnesses probably arose from the feeling that they were frail, not that their credibility was inferior to that of men, and that being frail they might not be able to stand up to the stringencies of the oath. Many terrible punishments were invoked in the oath for the perjurer, including "death by vomiting clots of blood and by inflammatory diseases," and "total destruction, as of an extinguished lamp, of children descendants, and property." These and many more punishments and curses, even more terrible, are inscribed in palm leaf and encased in beautiful red velvet, and the Buddhist witness in the courts today hold the Kyanza and promises to tell the truth, the whole truth. The pregnant Buddhist woman does not touch the Kyanza, but with palms together in prayerful respect, makes the pledge of truth to it.[3]

[1] E Maung, *Expansion of Burmese Buddhist Law;* lawyers are called 'Shay-nay' or Standers at the Front, in Burmese, or nicknamed, 'Shar-shay', the Long-Tongued.

[2] Shwe Yoe.

[3] *Burma Courts Manual*, Rangoon, 1960, p. 75.

Where there were no witnesses, the parties might submit to trial by ordeal. Four varieties of ordeal were noted in the Manugye: that by fire, that by water, that by molten lead, and that by rice – where the parties had to chew one tical of rice, he who finished first being declared winner. A trial by ordial was a solemn ceremony, and people would come to watch it, and the winner would go home "making the heavens ring with the news of his triumph, to the sound of martial music."[1] In the interests of public tranquility, however, ordeals were avoided if other means of discovering the facts and reaching just decisions could be found.

Criminal justice was an administrative function, and there was the notion of the King's Peace, to be kept by the punishment of offenders against the state, of those who committed murder, rape, abduction, robbery, theft, and grave scandal. The two areas – civil justice, and criminal – unavoidably overlapped as officials in the city and at the court of the King performed dual functions as administrator and judge, but the theory of separation was maintained. An edict of King Thalunmintra, issued in 1637 A.D., warned administrative officials against meddling in matters of civil justice. A suit for debt did not become a criminal case, the edict pointed out, just because the creditor was a minister or a high official. "Let not administrative officials seek to interfere by putting Our subjects who are being sued in irons or by taking them into custody."[2] A warning was added that those who did interfere and oppress would not get a second chance to do so.

At the commencement of each reign edicts would prescribe criminal offences, and their punishments. Whipping, confinement in irons, maiming, and banishment were some of the penalities. There were some more imaginative – and effective penalities too, such as blackening the face of a thief with soot and leading him round the town, his crime being proclaimed by beat of gong at the street corners. Capital punishment was rare, for it was felt that no man had the right to extinguish another human life, that what a man did in one existence he himself must pay for in the next and to judge him and sentence him was to offend the inexorable law of *karma*. "A King who does not put a murderer to death will be praised by the good spirits and all good men, and will be supported and assisted by them, while all evil beings who have no respect for the laws will keep afar off." So said Manu. "As *karma*

[1] Sangermano, pp. 86–90; Michael Symes, *An Account of an Embassy to Ava in 1795*, London, 1800, p. 476, for description of a trial by ordeal with wax-candles.
[2] E Maung, *Expansion of Burmese Buddhist Law.*

acts as judge, there was no need for an earthly judge to do more than protect without punishing, and a ruler who took upon himself to pass the sentence of death would himself in future existences suffer the misery resulting from manslaughter. Burmese rulers therefore refrained devoutly from passing the sentence of death. But they said, 'Let him travel by the usual road,' and they said it often."[1] The Kings said that quite often when court politics seemed to advise the removal of princes and contenders. In other cases, however, mercy was generously shown, and when a reduction of the sentence, or a pardon did not come promptly from the King, the Buddhist priests would put in their plea for mercy or ask the King to give them the condemned life as a royal alm. Capital punishment had become so rare in theory that in the last reigns of the Kings at Mandalay, when the British in lower Burma demanded the execution of a man who had murdered one of their political officers in Burmese territory, the Burmese ministers at Mandalay quietly replied that Burmese law and custom did not permit executions.[2]

That was Burmese society, its law and custom, along the ages, revolving round the village and the family. In some ways the society has changed little. But the world which was so far away from Mandalay knocked on the door, and came crashing in, and life could not remain quite the same.

[1] Harvey, *History of Burma*, p. 353.
[2] *Selections from the Records of the Hluttaw*, Rangoon, 1889, which also reproduces some edicts of King Thibaw relating to judicial procedure.

CHAPTER TWO

IMPACT OF BRITISH LAW

1. THE RULE OF LAW

British rule came to Burma in three stages: in 1824 when the lower maritime areas were taken by conquest; in 1852 when territory further north was seized and 'Lower Burma' became 'British Burma'; in 1885 when Upper Burma was annexed and the entire country consolidated as a province of the British Indian empire.

The problem that confronted the British at Mandalay was that of fashioning an administration that could be popular and workable at the same time. There were thoughts of establishing Burma as a protectorate with as its nominal head a prince who would be weak enough to submit to British guidance and yet of sufficient stature to win the respect of the people. But candidates who could satisfy those hard tests were not around. Strong princes, potential rivals, had been sent to travel "the usual road" in Thibaw's time; those who were quick enough had fled. There were also thoughts of ruling through the Hluttaw, but that was a peculiarly Burmese instutition which drew its life and meaning from royalty. Members of the Hluttaw did not come from an aristocracy; they were not professional judges, lawyers, or administrators, and when the King, their creator, faded from the scene, they also melted away, and an alien government could not breathe life into the Hluttaw again.[1]

Thus, gradually, it was the usual British colonial government that came be to built in Burma. With their genius for improvisation, their respect for history and traditions, their own and those that they found, the British began to build that pattern over the decades. Their's was not a policy to subdue and extinguish by fire and sword. The war of pacification was long – Burmese nationalism and sentiment for royalty proved stronger than anticipated – but the consistent aim was to restore peace and achieve harmony. Colonial wars worried the British conscience, and even though they served, at first, the interests of the business houses in London or Glasgow, when they were prolonged, business also

[1] John Cady, *A History of Modern Burma*, Cornell University Press, 1958; F. S. V. Donnison, *Public Administration in Burma*, London, 1953; Maung Maung, *Burma in the Family of Nations*, Amsterdam, 1957; Dorothy Woodman, *The Making of Burma*, London, 1962.

bled. Burmese society was not entirely shattered by the change at Mandalay. It had, all through the centuries, revolved round the family and the village, and these social units survived. The people "were very conscious of their relationship as 'sons of the village', their law was the law of custom and tradition, there were no great social differences, all bore their share in manning the village defences and in repairing the village wells or roads; it was a democratic little world ... and much of the traditions of past times remain alive today, village democracy, patriotism, and proud memories of independence back to the dawn of the Burmese race."[1]

Government became more organized and certain, however; its net spread out and covered the land. There were a few years, at first, of groping and adventure, but the fashioning of Leviathan proceeded firm and sure. Thus, when the maritime provinces were annexed, Mr. A. D. Maingy, appointed commissioner for Mergui and Tavoy at the lower ends of the country, was accountable to the Hon. the Governor of Prince of Wales Island, but was otherwise on his own, judge and administrator rolled in one, "to provide the people with a civil and political administration on the most liberal and equitable principles." In his first proclamation made on assumption of office, Mr. Maingy promised the people: "Rest assured that your wives and children shall be defended against all foreign and domestic enemies. That life and property shall enjoy every liberty and protection, and that your religion shall be respected and your priests and religious edifices secured from every insult and injury. Proper measures shall be immediately adopted for administering justice to you according to your own established laws so far as they do not militate against the principles of humanity and natural equity." Mr. Maingy also opened access to him "at all hours and places to any, even the poorest inhabitants, who may have business with me."

The first years were happy ones for Mr. Maingy. He found he could not understand Burmese judicial procedure; he abolished it. Civil suits were heard verbally, but 'professional pleaders' were not allowed, for they only complicated matters, and Mr. Maingy disliked complications. The parties were examined, and the witnesses, by oath or otherwise, as deemed most expedient, and then a brief abstract of the pleadings and the decision was recorded. Costs were levied at one-tenth of the value of the suit; if a claim was considered

[1] Hugh Tinker, "A Short Survey of Burmese History," *The Guardian*, English-language monthly magazine, Rangoon, December, 1961.

to be frivolous, the plaintiff had to pay one-fifth of the amount claimed as compensation. If, however, the parties compromised, even on the 'suggestion' of the Court, the full amount of the costs was remitted. Criminal charges were disposed of on similar lines, and were not carefully distinguished from civil claims. The policy was to discourage unnecessary litigation, and to dispense justice with the minimum of form. In this Mr. Maingy succeeded, and, though he did not know it, made a happy blend of British and Burmese notions of justice.

Leviathan could not be held off forever, however, and in 1834, Mr. Blundell, who succeeded Mr. Maingy, was reporting to the High Court in Calcutta of his fears that the Judges might "have in contemplation to introduce a closer analogy to the system of the Courts in Bengal which seemed unsuited to the state of society in these province... it would be likely to prove extremely unpalatable to a people accustomed under their former rulers to an expeditious and unencumbered though certainly corrupt administration of justice, and, since they have been under us, to an equally expeditious, though upright and impartial, settlement of their mostly unimportant cases." Mr. Blundell had his strongest protests reserved for the matter of admission of lawyers, which would "raise up a set of low adventurers seeking a livelihood by conducting cases on speculative terms," and also "strike at the root of our policy to discourage litigation, and encourage the prompt settlement of disputes."[1]

The High Court in Calcutta claimed, and won, its jurisdiction, however, and forms and procedures were introduced, as were lawyers, and the hierarchy of courts grew. Administration in general, and of justice in particular, became more organized and formal, more "impartial and objective." The change came to be felt more keenly at first in forms and procedures, rather than in substance. The impartial justice that the British introduced was identified with forms, which, as they grew more elaborate and technical, enlarged the role of lawyers, gave rise to court petitioners and touts, and pushed litigants – much against their better judgements sometimes – through the different appellate channels that

[1] J. S. Furnivall, "The Fashioning of the Leviathan," *JBRS*, April, 1939; Sangermano had this to say at page 86 of his book on the expeditious disposal of cases under the Kings: "In civil causes, lawsuits are terminated much more expeditiously than is generally the case in our part of the world, provided always that the litigants are not rich; for then the affair is extremely long, and sometimes never concluded at all. I was myself acquainted with two rich European merchants and shipmasters, who ruined themselves so completely by a lawsuit, that they became destitute of the common necessities of life, and the lawsuit withal was not decided, nor ever will be."

were opened as of course. Courts were, on the one hand, formal and forbidding, and on the other tempting and challenging to the pugnacious trait and the gambling spirit in the Burmese character.

As the civil service and the hierarchy of courts were established, the role of the village headman and the elders suffered reduction. Before, keeping peace and harmony in the village was not just a noble deed but had economic incentives also, for if the elders wanted "to wax fat they must keep as many villagers as possible, and to do this they must keep the peace and reduce quarrelsome litigation to a minimum. For this reason it will be found that in awarding punishment for an offence the elders rarely inflict the maximum penalty applicable. Because they have to live with both parties to the case their main objective is restoration of harmony, the granting of just sufficient economic balm to assuage the wounded without permanently antagonising the wounder. To this end they take into account not only the facts of the offence itself but also the age, sex, rank, wealth and kinship groupings of the contending parties, the likelihood of emigration of disaffected persons, and other factors known only to those having an intimate day to day contact with all concerned. Thus their orders were always placatory – the sublimation of that genius for compromise once believed the hallmark only of Perfide Albion."[1] With the change in the village and agricultural land system, the role of the headman was reduced to collector of revenue and upholder of the Village Act, directed in the main against disorder by imposing pains and penalties on the headman himself and the villagers if they failed to perform prescribed duties. "If," said Sir Charles Croswaite who had much to do with the pacification of the country, "we are to rule the country cheaply and efficiently, and to keep the people from being robbed and oppressed by the criminal classes, the village system must be maintained in vigour."[2] This policy emphasised the self-policing functions of the village, and neglected its role as a social system.

The "rule of law" that British rule established, and left behind as a legacy when Burma became independent, has, thus, come to mean many things. It has come to mean, on the merit side, equality before the law, fair play, uniformity of laws for all – private citizen and public official alike. It also means that disputes and differences that are amenable to legal settlement will be taken to the courts and peaceably settled,

[1] H. N. C. Stevenson, *The Central Chin Tribes*, Bombay, 1943.

[2] *The First Interim Report of the Administration Reorganization Committee*, Rangoon, 1949; Sir Charles Croswaite, *The Pacification of Burma*, London, 1912.

and that they will not lead to violence.[1] These virtues of the rule of law are most highly extolled today, and kept alive, to the extent that values can be given life in statutes, in the constitution and the laws. These are the values and virtues which U Nu pledged himself to uphold and perpetuate when he returned, in 1960, to the premiership, after the party and himself, and the constitution, had gone through more than a decade of hard tests.

"The first essential condition for making democracy secure in our lives," said U Nu in his address to Parliament, "is to base all our activities firmly on the rule of law. There are two kinds of laws which operate in this context: those that guarantee the freedom and equality of the individual against violation by the State; and those that ensure that individual freedom is exercised without affecting the rights and freedom of one's neighbours or the orderly working of society. We believe that the constitution, and other laws that already exist in the statute book, provide adequately in this respect, and that it is more in their application than in their absence, that there have been shortcomings in the past. For democracy to work, it is necessary not only that such laws exist but also that every citizen obeys the laws freely and conscientiously and that there is not only no disobedience but also no evasion. It is equally necessary that those in power enforce their authority through the rule of law, and not through fear or at the point of the bayonet. For democracy to work, this sense of the rule of law must be created in the minds of both the ruler and the ruled, and there must be constant effort to develop it and strengthen it, until it becomes a part of our very life and thought."[2] These remarks were noticed with approval by the Supreme Court in a case in which it set free by writ of *habeas corpus* a man who had been placed under preventive detention by the Government.[3]

The rule of law has also come to acquire other meanings. It is identified with form and technicality. "The Burmese people feel," as a scholar complained to a Reforms Committee, "that there is too much of logic and too much of hair-splitting in the system of British law, and too

[1] "There can never be two sets of law, one for those within and one for those outside the ruling party; whoever breaks the law must take the consequences. I myself, though Prime Minister, and president of the party, cannot escape punishment if I commit acts of lawlessness." So said U Nu in a broadcast talk on March 12, 1948, soon after independence, when elements of the party broke up printing presses of newspapers which had offended them. *Towards Peace and Democracy*, speeches of U Nu, Rangoon, 1949.

[2] Chamber of Deputies, *Proceedings*, April 5, 1960, reproduced in English translation in *Burma*, 13th. anniversary number, Rangoon, 1961.

[3] *Lim Lyam Hwat vs. Secretary, Home Ministry*, 1960 BLR 128 sc.

many loop-holes and too many occasions for the benefit of the doubt. So the lawless people, the offenders, who are sharper, enjoy the advantage."[1] Impartiality and detachment, which the rule of law demands in some degree, can easily degenerate into lack of sympathy and soul. Most of the British administrators "whilst discharging their duties conscientiously, did so with an air of detachment, and never forgot the vast difference between themselves and the Burmese," a British barrister wrote, "and the bond of human sympathy was lacking. Hence, the British administration, efficient within limits, was soul-less. It had the respect of those it governed for its good qualities, but they were not enamoured of it."[2]

Law and order is often equated with the rule of law, and in that equation the punitive and deterrent functions of law tend to be overemphasised. In Parliament, when "emergency powers" are demanded by the Government so that it may uphold the "rule of law", the justification invariably is that legislative sanction for such powers is granted by proper procedure; rule of law is therefore observed both in the motives for the legislation and in the processes that are employed for the legislation.[3] The dangers of using the expression to sanctify formal law and procedure, and extend the supremacy of the courts beyond reasonable limits, were also pointed out by Furnivall. Laws are made for men, and not men for laws; the rule, and supremacy of law, must not become the supremacy of the courts and the lawyers. "Judicial interpretation in pre-war Burma, " Furnivall wrote, "was to favour private interest over social welfare. This was a heritage from the British legal system which had been transplanted in Burma by judges and lawyers, either British or called to the English bar. But judicial traditions that fortified the national solidarity of England furthered the disintegration of social order in Burma." Now that Burma is free, he argued, social welfare must be the guide to judicial conscience in the interpretation of the law, and the legal constitution of the country should faithfully reflect the social and economic constitution.[4] A similar sentiment was expressed in a note of dissent which a Burmese political leader wrote for the report on reorganization of the administration: "It has been found that the introduction of the rule of law which is alien to Burmese tradi-

[1] Burma Reforms Committee, *Record of Evidence*, II, p. 73, Rangoon, 1922.

[2] E. C. V. Foucar, *I Lived in Burma*, London, 1956, pp. 24–25.

[3] E. g. debate in the Chamber of Deputies, September 21, 1955, *Proceedings*, vol. 8 no. 22, pp. 1475–1489, on law revision, and the Government's emphasis on its observance of the "rule of law".

[4] Furnivall in foreword to *Burma's Constitution*, by Maung Maung, The Hague, 1961.

tion has led to the disintegration of Burmese social life. An unalloyed continuance of the rule of law will further disintegrate Burmese social life. Hence any measure to reintegrate Burmese social life will have to depend more on social sanction than on the rule of law. I do not recommend that the rule of law should be dispensed with. But the rule of law should be adjusted in such a way that it should leave the largest possible scope to the play of social sanction."[1]

The above note only reopens, and does not settle, the whole problem of the meaning and function of law itself. If the rule of law means rule *by* laws, and nothing more, does it not stand in danger of becoming mechanical as rule by laws which are turned out as from a legislative factory? "If the devil can quote Scripture he can also cloak his activities in the habiliments of law. No systems of government have made a greater show of legalism than the communist and fascist dictatorships of recent date... Law is founded on morality, and morality finds its foundation in the moral integrity of the individual. Destroy this and we destroy morality. Destroy morality and we destroy law."[2] Yet, moral law and natural law, or morality, can be vague terms, and who is to be the judge of morality at any given time? Is he to be the judge on the bench, the legislator in parliament, or the vague collective person called the people – in whom modern written constitutions grandly vest the 'sovereignty of the state'? Thus, the search and the argument go on, and all that is clear is that law is not, or must not be reduced to, mere words in statute books and legal decisions, but is, or should be, an active, ceaseless social process that runs like a nerve system in the living society. Living laws are needed for a living society, and the bloodstream of law needs to be constantly renewed and nourished so that it may accomodate change in its continuity, youth in its age.

2. CODES AND COURTS

British rule did not deliberately set out to impose the British legal system on Burma. Liberal policy and *laissez faire*, and the social conscience of the British which might permit them to extend their rule over other lands and peoples but only in a gentlemanly manner, all

[1] *The First Interim Report*, Administration Reorganization Committee, Bo Khin Gale's note of dissent.

[2] A. Whitney Griswold, *Liberal Education & the Democratic Society*, Yale, 1959, chapter on *The Basis of a Rule of Law*.

these led them to first try and see if they could not preserve and work with existing systems. "It would have been open to the British Government," observed the Privy Council, "to adopt the ancient practice of issuing a fresh and authoritative Code. But it was more in accord with the genius and practice of the extension of British rule and of the incorporation of various races and populations within the British empire to accept the native laws in their main elements in so far they contained a working system of jurisprudence which was in accord with the traditions and habits of the people."[1]

Difficulty was encountered, however, in discovering what the Burmese system was, and what the Burmese customary laws were. Diligent studies and surveys were made, Burmese elders and scholars were consulted, and the Dhammathats compiled and translated. Manugye was translated by Dr. Richardson in 1847; extracts from the Dhammathats and existing customs were collected and published by Major Sparks in 1860; important Dhammathats in their Burmese and Pali texts were published under the auspices of Mr. Justice Sandford in 1877. Sir John Jardine, Judicial Commissioner of Lower Burma, was perhaps foremost among the British administrators and judges who tried to discover and preserve the customary laws. As president of the Educational Syndicate, an agency founded to promote higher education, and a forerunner of the Rangoon University, Jardine was able to marshal to the task scholars such as Dr. Forchhammer, Professor of Pali, and Bishop Bigandet, scholar in Buddhism. Jardine's circulars to judges and magistrates, embodying from time to time, the fruits of the researches, and his thoughts and comments, later published as Notes on Buddhist Law, early became classic commentaries on the subject. The search went far and wide, often into history and literature, sometimes into the depths of Buddhist philosophy.[2]

Sometimes the search would go in circles. As Jardine noted: "I have often had the following dialogue with Burmese judges – *Question:* What is the custom of the Burmans in the present times about such and such a matter (of inheritance or marriage law)? *Answer:* It is such and such. *Q:* How do you know that such a custom exists? Did you

[1] *Ma Hnin Bwin vs. U Shwe Gon.*

[2] Thus, for example, in an early case where the question was whether a Muhammedan was guilty of adultery, the opinions of leading Muhammedan moulvies in Rangoon were sought and texts on Buddhism read, to reach the decision that there was no adultery for there was no valid marriage with the Buddhist woman, who did not have a heavenly or revealed religion and a kitab, and did not believe in one God, but only in Nirvana, the 'perfect peace, goodness and wisdom'. *Printed Judgements, Judicial Commissioner for Lower Burma*, Rangoon, 1905, p. 607.

ever hear of an instance? *A:* No; but I say it is the present custom because it is stated as the rule of law in a Dhammathat of the last century."[1] But Dhammathats were often conflicting, sometimes obsolete in parts; memories also could fade about some matters. "These facts," Jardine noted, "account for the slight knowledge of Buddhist law possessed by most Englishmen, and for the hazy and contradictory opinions expressed on very common and simple topics by our Burman judges. A generation has passed away, and with it have disappeared the vivid recollection of older custom and the commoner knowledge of Pali which native rule fostered, while the oral traditions of the Burmese jurists must have been overlaid by the maxims of English courts."[2] The search could also go off the mark as it concentrated occasionally in the wrong places, such as when the Courts "looked for law about divorce in the wrong place, and raised inferences contrary to positive rules found elsewhere."[3] These dangers were recognized, and Justice Jardine warned, in a decision, that "it is the function of the Courts to know the present custom of the people so as to avoid the administration of long forgotten law... and here as in India the customs are changing. Knowledge of the present ought to go with the learning of the books."[4]

Another problem that appeared early was that of harmonizing tradition with progress, custom with change. The opening up of Burma was rapid; the building of roads and railways, the removal of barriers between 'British Burma' and 'Burmese Burma', the transition from armed peace to conditions of near normalcy and relative law and order, all these stimulated the flow of populations, the growth of new towns and cities, and trade of increasing volume and variety. The opening up of the Suez canal brought Burma nearer to Europe, made Burmese rice and minerals exportable commodities for the world markets. All these created situations which the customary laws were not adequately prepared to cope with. "The Burmese law was eminently suitable to an isolated agricultural people among whom riches were rare, the scale of whose commercial activities was small, and their tempo slow. The British occupation brought great economic changes. Foreign trade increased; the Indian moneylender financed the conversion of waste into cultivable land, and cash crops grown on it were milled for export in newly-erected steam mills; conservancy of forests to stimulate the

[1] Preface to *Wagaru Dhammathat*, Rangoon, 1892.
[2] *Notes on Buddhist Law*, III, p. i.
[3] *ibid.*, II, p. 4.
[4] *Ma Le vs. Ma Pauk Pin*, quoted in Chan Toon's *Principles of Buddhist Law*.

export trade in timber required new restrictive forest laws; communications were improved by the construction of roads and railways, and steamers appeared on the rivers. But the Burmese did not secure the full benefit of these new activities; lack of training and experience deprived them of the change of participating in the technical side of these activities, and the able, educated Burman preferred government service to commercial administration. There were increased opportunities for small scale trading, but the Burmese trader had little conception of the large capital necessary for successfully carrying on a modern business. Nowhere in Burmese law is there any vestige of the concept of a corporation, and a contract is enforceable if it is just, not because it is legally binding. Despite the basic similarity of the concept of negligence in the English and the Burmese systems, and although in both, it operated in substantially the same field, the rules governing contract and sale in Burmese law were unsuitable for international commerce in the 19th. century."[1]

Thus, gradually, the statutory laws which were designed on the British common law models for use in India were extended to Burma as well. The Contract Act, The Negotiable Instruments Act and the Trusts Act came to be formally extended to Rangoon even before the turn of the 19th. century, while these and other Indian codes were freely used as guides by judges and magistrates in other cities where they had no formal application. The Transfer of Property Act, relating to immoveable property, and the Sale of Goods Act, dealing with moveable property, came into force in Burma in 1924 and 1930 respectively. The Indian Penal Code, drafted and adopted in 1860, the Indian Evidence Act of 1872, and the Criminal Procedure Code of 1882 and 1898 were also among the earlier imports from India. By the early 1920's when judicial administration had become well organized in the country, the wholesale adoption of codes made for India on British common law principles was just about complete.

The organization of the courts proceeded at first in haphazard fashion as Burma was added piecemeal to the Indian empire. The first territories that came under British power were administered from Bengal, and when the Lieutenant-Governorship of Bengal was formed in 1854, the Burmese territories were placed under the Governor-General in Council. In 1862 the province of 'British Burma' was formed under a Chief Commissioner and when Mandalay also fell, the Upper Burma Laws Act of 1886 named the freshly acquired territories as 'Upper

[1] A. Gledhill, *Burmese Law in the 19th. Century*, a paper made available by the author.

Burma' and the older possessions as 'Lower Burma', and the whole province as 'Burma'. Some frontier and hill areas were formed as separate political and administrative entities. Thus the Shan State was given its own system, and its customary laws kept alive in wider areas than in 'Burma proper'. The Arakan hill tracts, the Chin hills, and the Kachin hill tracts, were also separate, under special administrative systems and with their customary laws and simple regulations forming the body of laws applicable in each area. In the entire province the executive officer was both judge and administrator in the early years, and these Maingy's and Blundell's enjoyed large discretion in the performance of their dual functions. Exept for the Recorders' Courts established in the seaport towns of Moulmein and Rangoon with English barristers as presiding judges, and the Small Cause Courts, the court system consisted of executive officers exercising prescribed civil and criminal powers, with the Deputy Commissioner as head of the district and chief appellate authority for decisions passed down by subordinate officers in his district. Commissioners, as heads of divisions or clusters of districts, exercised original civil and criminal jurisdictions, and appellate jurisdiction over cases decided in the districts as well. Thus the hierarchy went way out to the superior courts in Bengal with their final appellate and supervisory powers until they were transferred in large measure to the Chief Commissioner of British Burma. This was the basic system of courts which was formally recognized by Act I of 1863 passed by the Legislature in India, which also extended the Civil Procedure Code and the Limitation Act to the province.

The Court of the Judicial Commissioner was established by Act VII of 1872 to relieve the Chief Commissioner of his judicial functions, and a Special Court composed of the Judicial Commissioner and the Recorder of Rangoon exercised most of the powers of an Indian High Court over Lower Burma. The Lower Burma Courts Act, No. VI of 1900, formally merged the Courts of the Judicial Commissioner and the Recorder into the Chief Court of Lower Burma as the highest civil appellate court and the highest court of criminal appeal and revision. The Upper Burma Civil Courts Regulations, 1896, established the Court of the Judicial Commissioner for Upper Burma with all the powers of "a High Court established under Statute 24 and 25, Victoria, chapter 104" and as the court of final jurisdiction throughout the area to which the Regulations applied. By Letters Patent, 1922, the High Court of Judicature at Rangoon was established consolidating the powers and jurisdictions of the Chief Court of Lower Burma and the Judicial Commissioner of Upper Burma.[1]

The codes of law which were imported wholesale into Burma from India, first as unofficial guides and later by formal extension, embodied in large measures the principles of the British common law. In India, even more than in Burma, the British found a perplexing medley of laws "widely differing from each other but coexisting and coequal," as Lord Macaulay, the principal draughtsman of the codes described, and his answer was simple: codification on the principle of "uniformity when you can have it; diversity when you must have it; but, in all cases certainty." Sir Henry Maine saw in the medley a vast emptiness: "regard being had to its moral and material needs, India was a country singularly empty of law." The inevitable result was that the courts had to legislate to fill with British common law principles the "vast gaps and interspaces in the substantive law."[2] Burma received from India both the codes and the judicial interpretations, and thus received the British common law somewhat second-hand. Legislation for Burma was done in India for several decades, and by the time legislative powers passed to councils in Burma the import of the codes and the judicial principles from India was completed, and it was left to the highest courts in the country to harmonize as best as they could the imported laws and the indigenous laws and customs. "But the judicial system became more and more the apparatus of a foreign government. In the great majority of courts the law was administered by Burmese judges and magistrates, but on the bench they were living in a different world from that in which they lived at home. It was not that the judges could not apply the law, but as the law had no roots in the community, they applied it literally, mechanically. The British lawyers on the Chief Court also applied the law mechanically because they did not know the people. It had been alleged that there were no High Courts in the British empire where the atmosphere was so unreal."[3] Justice came to be identified more and more with formal laws and legal forms "devised originally for a different people in a different land and better suited to commerce than to agriculture," and the gap between "the law and the life of the people in Burma" appeared to widen with time.[4] Where,

[1] E Maung, J., in *Ma Thin vs. Maung Sei Tin*, 1949 BLR 74 S. C.; Donnison, *Public Administration in Burma;* Eggar, *Laws of India;* H. Cowell, *Constitution of Courts in India*, Tagore Law Lectures, Calcutta, 1872, pp. 243–246; *In re. Ma Mya vs. Ma Thein*, 4. Ran. 313, F. B.

[2] M. C. Setalvad, *The Common Law in India*, London, 1960, pp. 23 and 27.

[3] Furnivall, *Colonial Policy and Practice*, New York, 1956, p. 135.

[4] *First Interim Report of the Administration Reorganization Committee.*

however, the forms could be cut through or negotiated, and the inherent qualities of the British common law, such as commonsense and equity could be brought forth in full play, they found in Burmese notions of justice willing and eager partners.[1]

3. LIMITED ROLE FOR CUSTOMARY LAW

Customary law gradually came to be confined to affairs of the family mainly, and religious usage and instutitions. Because the British administrators identified it as having force among the Burmese who professed the Buddhist faith they called it 'Burmese Buddhist Law' and this name has passed into common use. The customary law of the Burmese was also identified as 'personal law' because "prima facie a Buddhist in Burma, irrespective of what his nationality is, and irrespective of whence he came, is governed by the Burmese Buddhist Law, i.e., by the Dhammathats and the precedents in the matter of marriage, inheritance and succession, unless he can prove that he is governed by a custom which has the force of law in Burma which is opposed to the Burmese Buddhist Law."[2]

The scope of customary law was larger when British rule began, but was reduced by the import of the codes from India. Thus, the Civil Code of the Province of Pegu, sanctioned in two parts in 1859 and 1860 by 'His Honour the President in Council' in India, stated in section I of part II that the Courts of Pegu "have always professed to administer Burmese Law, when the litigants belong to that race on all cases of marriage, seduction and adultery, divorce, adoption, inheritance, immoveable property." This scheme of administration of civil justice was developed further by Acts of 1872, 1875 and 1889, and the Burma Laws Act, 1898, which is still law today, in re-enacting similar provisions in the earlier Acts, vests force and validity in customary law in its section 13 thus: "Where in any suit or proceeding, it is necessary for any Court to decide any question regarding succession, inheritance, marriage or caste, or any religious usage or institution, the Buddhist Law in cases where the parties are Buddhists, shall form the rule of

[1] As Viscount Kilmur, Lord Chancellor of England, learned from his meetings with lawyers from all over the world, "in every kind of civilization the pursuit of justice is instinctive and a legal system which gives this instinct freedom to express itself has an inherent strength which is not easily destroyed." "Migration of the Common Law." *Law Quarterly Review*, January, 1960.

[2] Ba U, J., in *Daw Thike vs. Cyoung Ah Lin*, 1951 BLR 133 S. C.

decision, except in so far as such law has, by legislative enactment, been altered or abolished, or is opposed to any custom having the force of law." Sub-section 3 of the Act lays down that in cases which are not provided for by sub-section 1, or by any other enactment, the decision shall be according to "justice, equity and good conscience."

Caste does not exist in Burmese society. Religious usage and institutions are governed by their own rules and the Vinaya, while Buddhist priests keep strictly aloof from family and mundane affairs. 'Burmese Buddhist Law' therefore means, mainly, the customary law of the Burmese Buddhist family.

'Burmese' is the name for the majority race of Burma, as contrasted with the Shans, the Kachins, the Kayah, the Karens, the Chins, the Mon, the Arakanese, and such other minority races. 'Burman' is the generic term for all. The principles of 'Burmese Buddhist Law' have general application among the races, but many of the minority groups came under separate judicial and administrative systems under British rule, and their substantive and procedural laws were made up of prevailing local customs and simple regulations or orders issued from time to time. Thus, for example, section 11 of the Burma Laws Act, 1898, declared that "the law to be administered in a Shan State shall be the customary law of the State in so far as the punishments which may be awarded thereunder, or the practices which are permitted thereby, are in conformity with the spirit of the law in force in the rest of British India." The judicial system in the Shan States was prescribed later in the Shan States Civil Justice Order, 1900, and a Subsidiary Order, 1906, and these Orders and the customary law formed the *corpus juris* of the States through the decades and served quite well. Constitutional changes, and the move towards integration of the judicial system throughout the Union, have led the Shan State Council to make some amendments to the Orders by an Act of 1961, but the substantive laws remain unchanged basically.[1]

A "Buddhist" is one who accepts the three gems, the Buddha, the Law or Dhamma, and the Order of the priesthood or the Sangha, and lives by the teachings of the Buddha. Negatively, a Buddhist is one

[1] *Burma Gazette*, December 16, 1961. The Burma Laws Act, 1898, vested powers in the administration of civil and criminal justice in the Shan States in each chief of the state concerned, and a relinquishment of the hereditary powers by the chiefs in 1959, required the passage of The Burma Laws (Shan State) (Amendment) Act, 1959, to fill the gap. The States Courts Act, 1953, aims at providing a uniform system of administration of justice throughout the Union, but before it can come into full operation, the relinquishment of powers by the chiefs created a vacuum which had to be filled by the Act of 1961.

who does not have a heavenly or revealed religion and a kitab, who does not believe in one God, but only in Nirvana, "the perfect peace, goodness and wisdom."[1] Sincerity of belief, and devoutness are not the tests – for the Devil himself, leave alone the courts, knoweth not what is in the mind of a man or a woman – but it is the profession of one's faith that counts, and one's conduct in society as established by evidence. The question as to whether a man is a Buddhist or not has hardly ever troubled the courts, but the term 'Buddhist Law' used by the Burma Laws Act, and the more popular name 'Burmese Buddhist Law' have raised questions in the nature of conflicts in jurisdiction, such as whether 'Buddhist Law' applies to a Chinese in Burma who professes Buddhism. These questions have now been settled largely by judicial interpretation and by the enactment of special marriage laws for Buddhist women, as will be noticed in a later chapter.

In the first decades of British rule the administrators felt free in their choice of law in the performance of their judicial functions. The scholarly and the idealistic among them dug diligently to discover what Burmese customary law had to offer as guide to decision in particular cases. Even the gradual confinement of Burmese law to affairs of the family by the different Acts culminating in the Burma Laws Act did not unduly inhibit some of the judges. Thus, for example, in a case where the charge was kidnapping a Buddhist girl of under 16 years from her lawful guardianship with intent to have carnal knowledge, Justice Jardine felt it necessary to refer the case to the Special Court and to consult the Dhammathats before deciding that in Burmese custom consent of the parents or the guardian was essential for a man to marry a girl of 16, and as there was no such consent, an offence had been committed.[2] In another case where the accused was found cutting up the carcass of a dead bullock the day after it was missed, the Judge referred to the Manugye Dhammathat which "treats the flesh of a strayed or dead animal as property belonging to the owner to whom the herdsman, hirer, thief, or finder may have to account criminally or civilly"; the case was remanded to the lower court for further evidence to discover if the accused had tried to find the owner of the bullock, or report to the authorities first.[3] In the administration of criminal justice under the Penal Code and the Criminal Procedure Code extended from India, Justice Jardine warned his judges and magistrates that

[1] See footnote 2 on page 27.

[2] *Queen Emperor vs. Nga Ne U*, 1883, in Moyles, *Criminal Circulars, Lower Burma, 1872–1892*, Rangoon, vol. 1, p. 838.

[3] *Queen Emperor vs. Nga Chain*, 1883, Moyles, p. 902.

the law must not be rigidly enforced but considerations must be given to "humanity as well as equity and Buddhist law." He warned particularly that in the levy of fines by distress and sale of immoveable property belonging to the offender the separate property of the innocent husband or wife, or the share in the joint property, must not be seized as Buddhist law protected such property rights. "Otherwise," he warned, "there is danger of our British justice becoming unjust and of women being oppressed in defiance of the law of the country and the interpretations of the higher courts."[1]

As justice became more formal and organized, however, the habit of looking up Burmese law and custom in areas outside of those to which they were confined passed out of fashion. A narrower view came to be taken of law. The codes had arrived, and law was what they said it was. "Laws are rules of civil conduct enforced by the State," it was pronounced in a Full Bench decision of the High Court, "the only rules of Buddhist law enforceable by the State, according to the provisions of s. 13 of the Burma Laws Act, are those relating to succession, inheritance, marriage or any religious usage or institution. Other rules of Buddhist law cannot be juridically enforced."[2]

To sum up, 'Buddhist Law' or 'Burmese Buddhist Law' or more correctly 'Burmese Customary Law' applies among the Burmese who profess the Buddhist faith in subjects which are specified in S. 13 (1) of the Burma Laws Act. 'Buddhist Law', as that provision calls it, may be found in the Dhammathats and the treatises, the judicial decisions and precedents, old and new. Those are useful, however, in discovering what custom is that has acquired the force of law by ancient and universal usage. "Custom where it forms the rule of decision, does so not as a part of the Buddhist Law but in spite of and over-riding the rules of Buddhist Law. The relation between Buddhist Law and Custom having the force of law and over-riding the rules of Buddhist Law has a parallel in the relations between the original concept of English Common Law, as the general and common custom of the realm and particular custom – *legem et consuetudinem regni* of the early royal writs."[3] It is the living law of custom which is the law of the Burmese Buddhist family. To discover what that custom is in a particular case is, therefore, a burden of some weight on the judge and the lawyers who assist him. "The progress, welfare, and advancement of a democratic nation

[1] Circular memorandum 27 of 1881, Moyles, pp. 606–609.
[2] *U Pyinnya & Others vs. Maung Law*, 7 Ran. 677, F. B.
[3] E Maung, J., in *Dr. Tha Mya vs. Daw Khin Pu.*

depend, in a large measure, on judges. They can obstruct, frustrate, or give full effect to the will of a nation by their interpretation, exposition, and application of legal enactments." So observed Dr. Ba U, the first Chief Justice of the Union after independence. "Judges play an even more important role in the exposition of a personal law in cases where such law is not codified – as in the case of Burmese Buddhist Law – for this law is, in a way, judge-made law."[1] And because it is a living law which must depend for its growth on interpretation and application mainly, decision must be guided by a comparative examination of all the Dhammathats and literature available, a broad survey of the entire and related fields, and in the interpretation of the evidence "the principle of equitable construction, which is discountenanced in interpreting legislative enactments, cannot be excluded..."[2]

4. INTERNATIONAL LAW AND MUNICIPAL LAW

It is not in the customary law of the family alone, however, that the need for broad surveys, comparative studies, and liberal and equitable constructions appears to exist. The need is great, if not greater, in areas covered by the codes as well. The Burmese family goes on, and even though society changes, the blood bonds that bind the family preserve their strength and help to resolve the problems that rise within the family or from the changes in society. On the other hand, a modern, western-type constitution has been adopted in Burma, complete with popular assemblies, a central government, and a hierarchy of courts applying western contractual laws. The constitution is also pledged to "maintain social order on the basis of the eternal principles of justice, liberty and equality and guarantee and secure to all citizens justice social, economic and political, liberty of thought, expression, belief, faith, worship, vocation, association and action, equality of status, of opportunity and before the law." These pledges and aspirations expressed in the preamble are more specifically translated into guarantees of 'fundamental rights' in chapter II of the constitution and into 'directive principles' contained in chapter IV which do not have binding legal force yet but shall serve as 'the general guidance of the State.'

The values that are thus set as goals for society are neither new nor

[1] Dr. Ba U, *My Burma*, p. 112.
[2] E Maung, J., in *Dr. Tha Mya vs. Khin Pu.*

alien in that they are eternal and universal values. Yet the laws by which these values are to be given life and growth, and the machinery by which the laws must operate are old and outmoded. The laws and the machinery are not bad in themselves, but they tend to be static, and for change and growth they must rely mainly on Parliament which, in the first young years of a State, would tend to be preoccupied with its own forms and procedures, its own games, and, in the making of laws, would tend to swing between caution and conservatism in the interests of continuity, and impatient zeal to forge ahead with the 'revolution'. In Burma, thus, while Ministers and Government Members of Parliament have always gallantly stood up in the defence of 'existing laws' – namely the codes, orders, ordinances, and such, which were brought in from India from the early decades of the 19th. century till Burma's independence in 1948 by various means such as extension, adaptation, and adoption – the pace of legislative activity has also been fast since independence.[1] According to the National United Front, a research-minded opposition party, there were 141 days and 402 hours of effective sitting of Parliament in its term from 1956 to December 1959, and during that time 198 Acts were passed, thus making an average of 2 hours and 32 minutes of debate and discussion given to one Act.[2] Great improvements are being made to bring legislation and popular opinion closer: in the drafting of bills, for example, political parties work together sharing viewpoints and negotiating; draft bills are published to attract comments from the press and the public; seminars are conducted to debate the important features of the bills; special committees of experts are set up to study and report, and a standing advisory committee of learned elders gives its views on important public affairs.[3] Yet, to bring law and life into happier harmony, to make the aspirations of the constitution live, to get the 'existing laws' on the statute book to work and serve society as its strives for its goals, and to set new directions and create a living body of law so that there may not be any gap or vacuum, the Judiciary needs to take a broader, bolder view of its role and responsibilities. The High Court, and the

[1] Maung Maung, "The Search for Constitutionalism in Burma," *Indian Yearbook of International Affairs*, Madras, 1960.

[2] *ibid.* Also in Chamber of Deputies *proceedings* February 27, 1957, in which opposition members, in demanding longer sessions and more opportunity to debate, pointed out that between 1947 and 1956, a total of 660 Acts were passed in 600 days of effective sitting.

[3] An advisory committee headed by Dr. Ba U, one-time Chief Justice, and a former President of the Union, was appointed in April, 1960, soon after a new Government took office, and gave its views on subjects ranging from revision of mining regulations to the establishment of new states in the Union.

Supreme Court, the highest tribunals in the land whose law-making decisions are binding on the courts below, need to set their minds free and their aims high.[1] The Supreme Court has ruled that in interpreting the constitution, "construction most beneficial to the widest possible amplitude of its power should be adopted" so that the constitution, though written, may develop through usage and convention.[2] In another case in which the amount of damage awarded for defamation was at issue, the Supreme Court again held that decision must be guided not by narrow rules or mechanical interpretations, but by the widest considerations of the relevant facts, including social mores and cultures, the circumstances and backgrounds of the people involved, for no two people, nor two cases, could be entirely alike.[3]

The need for the Judiciary to consciously shape and mould the law – as a partner, not a usurper, of Parliament – is best illustrated by the somewhat peculiar situation that seems to exist in the relationship between international law and municipal law. The constitution, in section 211, "renounces war as an instrument of national policy, and accepts the generally recognized principles of international law as its rule of conduct in relation with foreign States." Section 212 "affirms its devotion to the ideal of peace and friendly co-operation amongst nations founded on international justice and morality." Yet, international law is not 'existing law' within the meaning of section 222 of the constitution.[4] And it has been held that as "it is by people who had lived or who had been trained under this system" – viz. that of enacted laws – "that the constitution was drawn up and enacted and it is therefore reasonable to conclude that when the constitution speaks of 'law' it speaks of the will of the legislature enacted in due form, provided that such enactment is within the competence of the legislature." It was also pointed out, with reference to the Burma Laws Act,

[1] Section 148 of the constitution erects the High Court and the Supreme Court as 'courts of record'; s. 152 makes 'the law declared by the Supreme Court... binding on... all courts within... the Union' in so far as it is applicable. A scale of weightage is in use for measuring the binding force of decisions. "Decisions of Their Lordships of the Privy Council on all Courts of the Province, decisions of the Full Bench of the High Court on all Courts, decisions of the Benches of the High Court on all single Judges and all inferior Courts, and decisions of single Judges on all inferior Courts..." *In re. Ma Mya vs. Ma Thein*, 4 Ran. 313, F. B. This scale is valid today, with the substitution of the Supreme Court for the Privy Council.

[2] *U Htwe vs. U Tun Ohn & One*, 1948 BLR 541, S. C.

[3] *U Saw Han vs. U Ohn Khin & 3 Others*, 1959 BLR 24, S. C.

[4] s. 222 (1) defines 'existing law' as "any law, Ordinance, byelaw, rule or regulation passed or made before the commencement of this Constitution by any legislature, authority or person in any territories included within the Union of Burma being a legislature, authority or person having power to make such law, Ordinance, Order, byelaw, rule or regulation..."

1898, and its predecessors, that "customary laws, the common law of England, and the principles of justice, equity and good conscience were not applied by their inherent force but were made applicable by enactment."[1]

International law, by this strict and narrow test, is not law because it is not enacted by Parliament, nor inherited as 'existing law'. It is largely, by this test, the customary law which guides the nations in their dealings with one another, and unlike the customary law of the Burmese family which draws its breath from statute and is better known and more certain, international law is not mentioned in the Burma Laws Act, is not enough known, and not easy to find. There is no denying that international law exists and that it is a good thing; the problem is to discover what it is, to distinguish between what is and what should be, to ascertain whether what should be is already what is. The folklore is that international law is no more than moral rules dressed up in judicial decisions and state practices which do not possess the full sanctity of law, and courts in Burma, anxious to preserve continuity, cling to positive, enacted law and fight shy of moral law or natural justice. "With changing social and political conditions notions regarding natural law change; all that remains constant is the appeal to something higher than positive law. Rules of natural law are the mirage which ever recedes from the traveller seeking to reach it. They are no doubt ideals to which positive law should strive to conform. But to accept natural law as a higher law which invalidates any inconsistent positive law would lead to chaos."[2]

When Burma was under British rule without separate international identity, international law questions did not frequently arise. World War II and military occupation by the Japanese forces raised a crop of questions. Burma was under occupation from May, 1942, to approximately May, 1945, during which period the Japanese first had a military administration and later, on August 1, 1943, proclaimed the independent status of the state within the 'Greater East Asia Co-prosperity Sphere'. By order of the military commander the courts were re-opened, after a few months of suspension, in 1942, and when independence was proclaimed they were slightly reorganized. All the time, however, the same laws were applied: the customary laws of the family, the British codes, and even the common law of England. The majority of the judges and magistrates who were appointed

[1] *Tinsa Maw Naing vs. The Commissioner of Police, Rangoon,* 1950 BLR 17, S. C.
[2] *ibid.*

under the occupation were the same people who had served before.

The competency of the courts and the validity of their judgements and decrees came up for determination very soon after the collapse of the military occupation, and the High Court had no difficulty in holding that the courts were competent and their judgements and decrees valid. Referring to Article 43 of the Hague Regulations, the High Court accepted that "an occupying power, while occupation lasts, is for all practical purposes the *de facto* Government, and its acts, legislative, executive, or judicial, consistent with the terms of Article 43, will be recognized by the legal Government." A competent court is, the High Court decided, "one which has legal authority to decide a case. Legal authority means authority under the laws of Burma. Occupation courts having been established under the municipal law of Burma, their judgements are valid and binding on the lawful Government." The High Court, in following Article 43 of the Hague Regulations, also felt it necessary to reiterate its approval of the British practice in which "international law has no validity in the Courts except in so far as its principles are accepted and adopted by the municipal law. The Hague Regulations will be treated as incorporated into the municipal law of Burma in so far as they are not inconsistent with the ordinary law of the country."[1]

The reorganization of the occupation courts, with some changes in jurisdiction and the establishment of a Supreme Court as the highest appellate court, was also held to be in order and within the powers of the military authorities, though the "so-called independent government of Burma, having been brought into existence during the War before the conclusion of peace or the signing of a treaty, had no legal status and new laws passed by them should be regarded as laws passed by the occupying power."[2] It was also held that the "Japanese military authorities acted in excess of their authority under international law in issuing a parallel system of currency to the currency established by the lawful Government," and that "Japanese so-called currency was never lawful currency in Burma, and a loan of Japanese notes was not loan of money."[3] The status of contracts, such as an agency contract, under the occupation, presented some difficulty after liberation. When

[1] *The King vs. Maung Hmin*, 1946 RLR 1 S. B.

[2] *ibid.* Also, *Maung Hla Maung vs. Ko Maung Maung*, 1947 RLR 1 F. B.; *U San Wa vs. U Ba Thin*, 1947 RLR 78 F. B.; E Maung, "*Enemy Legislation and Judgements in Burma*," 30 *Journal of Comparative Legislation & International Law*, 1948.

[3] *Ko Maung Tin vs. U Gon Man*, 1947 RLR 149 F. B.; *Dr. Chan Taik vs. A. M. Dooply*, 1948 BLR 454, also in *Annual Digest of Reports of International Law Cases*, 1948, p. 576.

the agent was in Burma and the principal in India, it was held that war and the occupation of Burma did not terminate the contract, that "such question is to be decided in accordance with the municipal law of Burma and not by international law... that the condition of Burma under Japanese occupation was peculiar and there is no Common Law authority on this point... while the municipal law is in consonance with the American decisions in *Kershaw vs. Kelsey*, 100 Mass. 561, and *Williams vs. Paine*, 169 U.S. 55." It was also pointed out that the declaration of war made by the 'independent' Government of Burma under Japanese power on Britain had no legal effect as there was not the 'necessary status' to declare war.[1] In another case where "the contract of agency was made in India and clearly meant to be performed in Burma" it was decided that the principle of *lex loci solutionis* should apply and the contract allowed to stand while leaving open "the larger question of the effect in general of war on contracts of agency when the line of war divides the principal from the agent."[2] The test of public policy and the interests of Burma was adopted by the High Court in examining another case in which the principals in India had contracted with their agents in Rangoon to carry on money-lending business. Again it was held that municipal law must govern decision, for the Burma Laws Act prescribed enforceable law for the land, and where there was a gap filled it with 'justice, equity and good conscience,' but as "international law deals with the question of the relations between states and not between individuals," the Contract Act and the Defence of Burma Act applied. Performance of the contract was not prohibited by the Acts in the situation created by war, and "by allowing trade and intercourse as in this case, the interests of Burma would not only be not injured but be promoted." The contract of agency, it was ruled, continued to be valid.[3]

The position of international law has become even less certain after Burma's re-emergence as a member of the family of nations. Despite sections 211 and 212 of the constitution which pledge acceptance of the 'generally recognized principles of international law' and devotion to the ideals of 'international justice and morality' when specific

[1] *Chettiar vs. Chettiar*, 1948 BLR 278, also 1948 *Annual Digest*, p. 537. The High Court in this case also noted the observations of the Supreme Court of the Occupation, in civil reference 2 of 1943, that "the national character of Burma and its people remains as it was before; consequently British Indian subjects living either in Burma or India cannot be treated as 'alien enemies' of this country."

[2] *Chettiar vs. Chettiar*, 1949 BLR 56, S. C., also in 1948 *Annual Digest*, p. 537.

[3] *Ramaswamy Iyengar vs. Velayudhan Chettiar*, 1952 BLR 25 S. C., also in 1956 *Annual Digest*, p. 754.

issues arise involving international law the search for that law tends to be limited to the narrow confines of the codes, and construction to be restrictive rather than liberal. A classic example is provided by *Kovtunenko vs. U Law Yone*, better know as the *Tass case*, in which the Supreme Court had to decide the question of sovereign immunities.

Kovtunenko was the representative of Tass, Soviet News Agency, in Rangoon, and U Law Yone the editor of *The Nation*, English-language newspaper. Tass news bulletin, which was circulated free to the press and other public information agencies in Rangoon, carried a news item with a Rangoon dateline, in which it was alleged that U Law Yone, and two other editors of important national newspapers, had received large gifts of money from the American Embassy. By common knowledge the Embassy limited its gifts to the local press, around the relevant time, to one bottle of whiskey per newspaper at Christmas, without discrimination, and the Tass correspondent himself was probably a recipient. U Law Yone, deeply and rightly offended, prosecuted Mr. Kovtunenko in the court of the District Magistrate on a charge of criminal libel. For some weeks criminal process failed to reach Mr. Kovtunenko, and during that time the Russian Embassy approached the Foreign Office with a request for intervention, furnishing a certificate that Tass was a part of the Soviet Government. Request denied, Mr. Kovtunenko, who at last put in a notional appearance in court through his lawyer and furnished bail, pleaded that he was protected by immunity. The District Magistrate rejected the plea, and Kovtunenko applied to the Supreme Court to issue a writ of certiorari and have the lower court proceedings quashed.

The Supreme Court rejected the application, and in a carefully thought out judgement reviewed the position of international law in the *corpus juris* of the State, somewhat regretfully noticing that the *corpus* was by no means full-bodied yet. "After a hundred years of British rule," observed the Court, "and trained in the law as we are according to Anglo-Saxon concepts, we tend to rely upon English and American authorities but in dealing with the matter before us, we must bear in mind that in the Anglo-American systems there is always the Common Law to rely upon and that international law is deemed to be a part of the law of the land." The Court pointed out that section 214 of the constitution requires parliamentary sanction to incorporate an international agreement in the body of the municipal law, and no such treaty or agreement has become part of the law of the land relative to international immunities.[1] It was held that even the acceptance of the 'generally recognized principles of international law' which section 211 provides for is not sufficient to import international law into the *corpus juris*. "It is, however, argued that because of s. 211... it should be taken that international law is recognized as part of the law of the land. It is an attractive proposition, but in our judgement, a rule of conduct that the Union Government should follow 'in its relation to foreign States' is not necessarily the procedure that a Burmese Court is to observe in the absence of specific enactment which would make such observance legal. We interpret the section to mean that it is a declaration of policy which provides guidance to Government in its international relations and makes it incumbent upon it to take such legislative measures as may be necessary to bring it into line with other States." In the result, the Supreme Court ruled that in the absence of legislative provisions to grant immunity from criminal process "no person, not even the President of the Union, merely by virtue of his status, can claim immunity from the penal laws of this country, and in so far as the Courts are concerned, a complaint of the nature involved in the present case will have to be dealt with according to law." It was hinted, however, that the Government might consider entering a *nolle prosequi*, and put an end to the whole disagreeable affair, for, the Court remarked, its ruling "does not mean that every alleged offender without exception, has to undergo the indignity of a trial, because it is within the competence of the executive to intervene by withdrawing the prosecution, a procedure which is often resorted to in many countries, on the ground of public policy."[2]

This note on the relation of international law and municipal law shows up the need to fill gaps in the 'law' and constantly help its growth.

[1] S. 214 reads: "No international agreement as such shall be part of the municipal law of the Union, save as may be determined by the Parliament." Burma was a party to the Geneva Convention on Diplomatic Immunities, and appropriate legislation will incorporate it into municipal law, as has been done with the agreement to extend privileges and immunities to personnel of the United Nations.

[2] *E. T. Kovtunenko vs. U Law Yone*, 1960 BLR 51 S.C., judgement rendered on March 1, 1960. The Government did finally enter a *nolle prosequi*, but previous to that the Prime Minister himself, at the request of the Soviet Government, let Kovtunenko leave the country on humanitarian grounds, as he pleaded illness. A citizen filed a charge that the Prime Minister was guilty of harbouring an offender, and when the charge was dismissed in the lower court, went up to the High Court, and finally the Supreme Court which pointed out that there was no intention to harbour, and "the action of the Prime Minister was the action of the Government as a whole, performed in the normal relations with a sovereign State. No act of State is justiciable and if there is real basis for an indictment against the Government it should be ventilated in the proper forum, the Parliament." *The Guardian*, English language newspaper, Rangoon, December 6, 1961.

Legislation is a means, and an important one, but by itself alone it is inadequate, and it is certainly not the only means for the development of law. From taking the restricted view that nothing is law unless it has a place in the statute book to assuming that all laws spring into life from mere entry into the book is but a step, and both views have their dangers. The Judiciary needs to take a bold hand in developing the law, by broad and liberal interpretation, by building a body of case law to harmonize the statutes and the living customs and changing circumstances of society. 'Justice, equity and good conscience' provide an ample reservoir of law, but for the law to live, for it to be the people's law, the notions of justice, equity and good conscience must be those of the people. To discover the notions and give them life and force, to guide and educate them where necessary, are tasks which offer both challenge and opportunity to the Government and the Judiciary alike, and to educators, officials and all those engaged in public service – private or governmental – as well.

CHAPTER THREE

THE BURMESE FAMILY

1. THE INDIVIDUAL

A consistent feature of the Burmese family has been the freedom of the individual. "The Burmese commoner chose as wife an equal, to be his helpmate; they shared their daily life, its common toil and interest; their children grew up under the care of an equal man, an equal woman, gaining the benefit of a father's as well as a mother's example."[1] The Dhammathats spoke of the power of the father over the children whom he might even sell into slavery, of the power of the husband, the lord and master, over his wife. But this power was more true in theory than in practice, and the descriptions of the power bore traces of Hindu law grafted on at random, and "our debt to Hindu law is not inconsederable but its extent can be, and has often been, exaggerated."[2] Thus it was warned in an early judicial decision that "the notions about *patria potestas* have changed and are changing; and the present tendency being to confer rights on individuals, the courts should be careful in dealing with the old rights and powers of parents as disclosed in the Dhammathats."[3]

The family is loosely knit by love and respect, not welded together by power. The father is the acknowledged head of the family, but when he is absent or gone, it is the mother who takes over. Sons under puberty and unmarried daughters below the age of 20 come under the care of the parents whose consent they need if they wish to launch out on their own, as in marriage. Yet, on them also, the power rests lightly, and it is more in the nature of filial love and duty.

Buddhism teaches that it is virtuous and good to respect the Buddha, the Law, the Sangha, teachers, and parents, and this lesson sinks deeply into the consciousness of a Buddhist boy who, by custom, spends a few months or years in a monastery, serving the priests and learning from them to read and write and to be a good Buddhist. Girls too learn this lesson at home, or the village school, and this deep feeling, rather than any 'positive law' or measured power, holds the family together. The

[1] Harvey, *History of Burma*, p. 210.
[2] E Maung, *Expansion of Burmese Buddhist Law*, chap. 3.
[3] Cited by Chan Toon in *Principles of Buddhist Law*, p. 25.

family may not live forever under one roof. On marriage the sons may leave and the daughters too, but where they go they take this feeling along, and it is customary for them, even when they reach advanced years, to inform, consult, or seek instructions from, their parents when they make important decisions in business or profession or family life. There is no system of the joint family in the Hindu sense, no patriach ruling over an expanding empire. Yet, the Burmese family too lives and expands to the very limits of that feeling's big embrace, and it is not unusual for a Burmese adult, man or woman, to describe his family – in filling, for example, the many forms and statements that modern life demands – as including his aged father and mother, his grandfather or maternal aunts and uncles.

Burmese society had been isolated and sheltered from the stresses and the furious march of the modern world, way back from its beginnings right down to British annexation, and then also the shock of change was as soft as it could be. The social fabric was not torn, the family went its ways. Perhaps it was the abundance of natural resources, the fertility of the land that gave enough for all to eat and get their simple basic needs and a little more besides for charity and the festivals after harvest, perhaps it was Buddhism which gave contentment, the people were happy, life was free and easy. But the Burman was "neither idle nor lazy," as a British administrator found. "When occasion demands he will work as hard as anyone. The farmer and fisherman each has seasons when he must rise up early and late take his rest. What the Burman does not care to do is to make toil a pleasure; to work merely for the sake of doing something or for the purpose of amassing wealth beyond his needs. With a fertile country, with no pressure of population on subsistence, with few wants, why should he strive or cry? For him progress and strenuous life in themselves have no attraction. We are trying to teach him our ideals, to show him how far superior is our civilization. When we shall have succeeded, we shall have spoilt the pleasantest country and the most delightful people in the world."[1]

That was when the 19th. century was coming to its close, and the population of Burma was, by the Census Report of 1891, about 7 million, of whom 6,888,075 persons were Buddhists, and the rest animists and worshippers of Nats.[2] Today the population is passing its 21 million mark; new ideas and ideologies, and the 'revolution of rising ex-

[1] Thirkell White, *A Civil Servant in Burma*, p. 47.
[2] Jardine in introduction to Sangermano's *The Burmese Empire*.

pectations' are coming in through the front as well as the back doors. How much of the rising expectations can be fulfilled at the sacrifice of how little of the old traditions and cultures poses both a problem and a challenge to the men of law and government and the social reformers of Burma.

Buddhism inspires individualism. It stresses the law of cause and effect in the revolving wheel of life in which the individual must work out his own release from the pain of birth and death to the state of calm and happiness. His life in this existence is the effect of the previous life that he had lived; what will follow in his next existence will reflect the good or the bad that he has done and is doing in this life. It is like the law in the natural sciences where energy invested is returned as energy in some form, but never destroyed, and in terms of measure the out-put and the in-put are the same. Thus it is that the individual in the Burmese family lives his or her pre-destined life, builds on his or her own for the next life into which he or she must migrate, and so on, endlessly until the tiresome journey is ended and Nirvana entered. This Buddhist philosophy and ethics run deep in the family and in society, and ritual is kept at a minimum for it has no meaning, and power, where it is acknowledged, is gently held for it has no permanence nor meaning either.

The Burmese family does not have a family name. The wife does not take her husband's name, but keeps her own, which she received when she was a few months old from her parents who had consulted the astrologers who in turn had probed into the secrets of her stars. The day she was born and the time she was born were relevant, and they went into her horoscope, the chart and symbols of which were believed to represent the map of her life. A horoscope is accepted by the courts as evidence of age, though the judges, not knowing the language of the stars, do not accept the map.

The names in the family are thus individual names, chosen solemnly with the help of the astrologers, or sometimes, in fond play by the parents who pick nicknames of affection which somehow endure through the lives of the Fat One, the Short One, the Tall One, the Plump Bottom, and dozens others which cause the wearers of the names an occasional blush in their advanced years. The bestowal of name on a child is done in quiet ceremony in which pickled tea is offered to the neighbours, some offerings made to the guardian Nats of the home, of the village or the town, and of the child whose journey in one life has begun. In later life a man or a woman may change his or her name without much formality, with no resort to courts, and the change calls for the offering of pickled tea to friends again. Pickled tea does indeed play a large part in Burmese social life.

Since nothing is permanent on this earth, the Burmese Buddhist family does not trouble itself with its perpetuation. In the Chinese family of old "there are four things which are unfilial, and the greatest of them is to have no posterity."[1] In the Hindu family too it was important to have certain rites and rituals performed by male heirs, mere women being inadequate, and marriage and adoption were institutions which often had the purpose of bringing males into the family. In the Burmese family rituals are absent, there is equality between husband and wife, sons and daughters, and as for perpetuity, why, the Buddha himself had to die.

2. HUSBAND AND WIFE

The Dhammathats – written by monks and men – sometimes describe the husband as the lord and master of the home, and the Burmese wife quietly keeps him thinking so, for it makes him feel happy and renders it easier for her to run the home.

"It is simply a part of good manners," notes a Burmese wife and scholar, "of what is pleasurable and seemly, to respect the person of a male, to give precedence to his manhood on all social occasions, and to attend to his wants. But in the all-important matters of money, of divorce, inheritance, of freedom of movement, the right of giving advice, of transacting business or of putting one's own name alongside a husband's on a shop front, women admit no inferiority. Thus they serve without shackles, and are equal without impairing the pride of masculinity."[2]

Another Burmese mother and scholar writes: "We like to give precedence to our men in our own homes because we acknowledge them, until their death, as head of the household.Possibly we can afford to offer them this courtesy because we are secure in our rights and status. But part of the deference we offer them stems from the influence of Buddhism in our country. We believe that when a new Buddha comes to the world it will be a man (though, to be sure, one of us who is now

[1] Mencius, IV A, 27.
[2] Mi Mi Khaing, "People of the Golden Land," Perspective of Burma, *Atlantic Monthly*, 1958; also her *Burmese Family*, Calcutta, 1946, for an intimate account of family life.

a woman may, in a later life, be born a man and eventually progress to Buddhahood)... Altogether, in our social life as well as in our public life we feel that we, as Burmese women, occupy a privileged and independent position. It is a position for which we are trained – almost imperceptibly, and with love and security – from childhood. It is a position which is not limited either by marriage or by motherhood, and which allows us, eventually, to fit ourselves into the life, the work, and all the rewards that our country has to offer equally with our men."[1]

Thus, in important matters – such as money – women enjoy equal rights as the men, and their only disadvantage seems to be that they cannot from womanhood rise direct to Buddha-hood, but nobody wants to become a Buddha, anyway, except in stereotyped prayers. The equality of women is recognized not in the home only, but in public life as well. Women enjoy constitutional rights of equality; in fact they helped to write constitutions. Women took their seats in Round Table conferences in London in the 1930's when constitutional reforms for Burma were discussed and drafted. Thus, Daw Mya Sein pointed out that from time immemorial Burmese women had played their parts in public life "as law-givers, as judges, as writers, as administrators, and as great philosophers," and demanded that new constitutions must recognize that fact.[2] Dr. Daw Saw Sa, another lady delegate to a later conference, declared that Burmese women "are fully emancipated and are regarded by men in our land as equal partners with them in the home, economic and political matters, as borne out by their unanimous and full support of our claims."[3] The gallant Burmese men on the delegation, and the chivalrous British gentlemen who sat round the table fully agreed that "the women of Burma occupy a position of freedom and independence not attained in other Provinces. Socially there is practical equality between the sexes; purdah is unknown; women take their full share with men in the ecomonic life of the country, and the percentage of literates among women is far higher than elsewhere. Adopting the recommended literacy test, and combining with it an age qualification for women of 21, it is proposed to raise the number of woman voters from 124,000 to about 700,000." The total electorate would then rise "from about 2.08 million (1,956,000 male and 124,000 female) in a population of 12.3 million to about

[1] Daw Mya Sein, "The Women of Burma," in *Perspective of Burma.*
[2] Burma Round Table Conference, *Proceedings*, Rangoon, 1932, p. 39.
[3] Indian Constitutional Reform, *Joint Committee Records*, London, 1934, vol. II.

3 million (2.3 million male and 700,000 female) in a population of 12.9 million." If the sharp rise in number of the female voters filled the hearts of the gentlemen at the meeting, Burmese and British, with fears, they had the good manners and good sense not to show them.[1]

In the drafting of the constitution in 1947 also women took a hand, and their interest was not limited only to the provisions which protected their equality.[2] In the matter of the franchise the minimum age was lowered to 18, and discrimination of all kinds – on grounds of sex, of property ownership, of literacy and education – were abolished.[3] Not only is the equality of women legally recognized, but women have in fact been participating actively in all areas of national life such as government and diplomacy, politics and parliament, the law, education, and even in the armed forces.

In the home, the wife is, by custom and law, a sharer, and not merely a bearer of the burden of household chores and of children. Her rights to her own separate property, which she brought to the marital home or acquires later, are well defined; her share in the husband's and the joint earnings is a vested right. When the husband is away, or dies, the headship of the family passes to her, not to the eldest son.

The Dhammathats had much to say about the happy home, the rights and duties of husbands and of wives, and to lend weight to the sayings, the authority of the Buddha was sometimes invoked. They read, however, more like moral teachings and folk wisdom which the Burmese family today accepts only in much diluted form. Thus the Manugye Dhammathat prescribes the five duties of a wife as "rising from bed before the husband rises; retiring to bed after he has done so; taking his instructions for her day's work; carrying out his behests according to his wishes; speaking to him in a pleasant and affectionate way; and providing against the inclemencies of the weather for the husband's comfort." The husband's 'good qualities' are described by the Kaingza Dhammathat as those of "striving to acquire wealth; providing the wife with a good house; maintaining the wife, children and slaves with

[1] *ibid.*, p. 15.

[2] Constitutional guarantees of equality may be found in s. 13 which prohibits discrimination; s. 14 which provides for equality of opportunity; s. 15 which guarantees 'the same pay... for similar work' as men; s. 76 (4) which gives equal right of vote or candidacy for Parliament.

[3] The minimum age of a candidate must be 21, while the voting age is 18. Parliamentary Elections Act, 1948, sections 11 and 23, to be read with s. 74 of the constitution.

tender watchfulness; looking after the cattle with care; supporting those of the relatives who are poor."[1] If the wife does not respect her husband who shows these qualities she shall be "criminally punished" but if he does not show these qualities "she may abuse him with impunity." But the wife is not a lesser person than the man because of her sex; in fact she may be nobler. Manugye prescribes this rule: "The husband and wife may be equal in personal appearance, age, wealth and rank, but if one surpasses the other in power and wisdom, the former shall be regarded as the nobler, and shall be respected by the latter."[2]

3. PARENTS AND CHILDREN

Children are born into the family, or brought into it from another marriage, or by adoption. These natural-born children, step-children, and adopted children have their rights and duties even as the parents have power over them and owe them duties. "In youth a person is under the guardianship and control of his or her parents; but when grown up he or she has to control himself or herself. In old age his or her children or grandchildren maintain and look after him or her."[3] This is a brief but fair statement of the reciprocal rights, duties and expectations that exist – today as strongly as ever before – between parents and children.

A child grows old slowly in the Burmese family. He may become an adult and a father, but in the eyes of the parents he remains a child. Puberty, when a son becomes competent and free to marry, generally marks his coming of age, but a girl remains longer under parental care and power. Twenty is the accepted age at which a girl is emancipated; to marry before she comes of age, she needs the consent of her parents, of the father specially, the Dhammathats say, though in fact it is the mother who usually prevails with her natural flair. "It is the duty of a man," warn the Dhammathats, "to give his children, grandchildren or slaves in marriage on their attaining the age of fifteen or sixteen years. Otherwise, if they fall into sin, he shall not take offence."[4] But that is a counsel of wisdom, not a binding obligation, and fifteen or sixteen is the age of a child when the parents begin to think of a family

[1] *Kinwunmingyi Digest*, II, p. 104–105.
[2] *ibid.*, p. 113.
[3] *ibid.*, p. 236.
[4] *ibid.*, p. 32.

for him or her. Marriages below that age are not common, and child marriages, which had to be restricted by law in India, never formed a feature of the Burmese family system.[1] Parents, like parents the world over, liked to arrange the marriages for their sons and daughters, and the go-between and the marriage market were operative well up to the start of World War II. The war broke up homes, scattered the sons who served in the army or sought their fortunes away from home, and the post-war years which have been seeing an increasing emergence of women into institutions of higher learning and public life, have put an end to the career of the go-between. Unfortunately for the go-between – who was generally a woman, for the job was delicate, and called for womanly delicacy and good taste – the boys and girls who go away early from their homes these days take their hearts with them and give them away freely, dispensing with the services of the traditional go-between, without as much as a "by your leave" to their parents. This situation was less frequent but not entirely unknown to the writers of the Dhammathats who, knowing the nature of woman, had said that if the parents took bridal gifts from a suitor and promised him their daughter's hand, and the girl was unwilling, all that the parents could do was return the gifts. It was Burmese equity at its best. "If a daughter desires to marry a man," the Dhammathats advised, "her parents should permit her to do so in order to prevent disgrace. If a young woman, without any sense of propriety visits her lover's house, her parents are scandalised thereby." To avoid scandal, the sensible thing to do is to give her the man she wants. Her preference weighs heavily, in fact is decisive. "If one son is presented at the time of bethrothal and another is substituted at the time of marriage, the bride may marry the one she prefers."[2] Or marry neither, and elope with the man she loves, and if she does that three times, even after the parents have tried to reclaim her, she breaks herself free from parental control and is free to marry him.

The Majority Act, a British statute made for India in 1875 and brought into Burma, fixes the age of majority for "persons domiciled in Burma" – male or female – at 18 in the absence of a guardian, or 21 if a guardian has been appointed or declared by a Court. This provision does not, however, govern marriage, dower, divorce and adoption, matters which fall within the province of customary law. The

[1] The Child Marriage Restraint Act is directed against marriages in which either of the parties is a 'child', meaning one who is under 18 if he is a male, or under 14, if she is a female.

[2] *Kinwunmingyi Digest*, II, p. 52.

Contract Act, a similar British statute, goes by the Majority Act to ascertain the age of competency to contract, and questions have arisen in Courts whether breach of promise to marry must be decided under the Contract Act or by customary law. These, and other conflicts in law, will be noticed in a later chapter.

CHAPTER FOUR

MARRIAGE

1. CELEBRATION AND PROOF

Marriage is a civil institution into which the Buddhist religious element enters not at all. "The very idea of wedlock and its attendant worldly life is opposed to the ultimate end of Buddhism – the annihilation of Desire; and notwithstanding that the Buddha, in his discourses to the laity, laid down rules of conduct to be observed by married persons, parents and children, yet he was careful to impress upon his hearers the need for keeping in mind the spiritual life. Thus, while commending him who supports his father, mother, wife and offspring, he at the same time indicates the goal of Nirvana, the striving for which must necessarily involve celibacy."[1]

The counsel of perfection that man should lead a life of celibacy and concentrate all of himself on the striving for Nirvana checked the spread of Buddhism in India, it has been said. "The elevation of woman (in Buddhism) is rather more perplexing as the theology treats marriage from the ascetic point of view: a wise man is to avoid it as if it were a burning pit of live coals, and to wander lonely on the path of life, like a rhinoceros. These counsels of perfection were met in India by the same sort of arguments that Chaucer puts into the mouth of the Wife of Bath in his Canterbury Tales. According to Monier-Williams they checked the spread of Buddhism. The people murmured and said, "Gaudama Buddha is come to bring childlessness among us, and widowhood and destruction of family life.' All the same, Buddhism admits of nuns and lay sisters; and its love of equality comes to their aid."[2]

Social life in Burma, and for that matter in the Southeast Asian countries where Buddhism is the religion of the majority, is so wrapped up in religious ethics that the absence of priests and religious elements from the ceremony of marriage becomes all the more remarkable. "Here no member of the Buddhist clergy officiates because the love is of a profane nature, and the contract purely a social one. But there are the go-between friends and relatives, busy making sure that both sides

[1] May Oung, *Leading Cases on Buddhist Law*, Rangoon, 1914, part I, p. 2.
[2] Jardine in introduction to Sangermano.

know what they are taking on, consulting with the local sages to see whether the horoscopes of bride and groom are well matched, choosing the most auspicious day and hour for the union, and selecting the most happily married couple of the family's acquaintance to lead the ceremony so that one successful marriage will bless another. The ceremony itself is a beautiful one, full of a simple but moving symbolism. The hands of bride and groom are joined and bound together with a silk scarf. They partake of food from the same bowls and make obeisance together. The guests bring gifts of money to help in setting up the new household. And finally, there may be a playful pantomime in which the groom's friends must bargain with the bride's friends to allow him to enter her room."[1] At night the male friends of the couple may come and throw a stone or two on to the roof of the bridal home, demanding once again their 'stone fee' or *ge-bo*, a small bribe the young couple must offer to induce their friends to leave them in peace. Partly also this custom is a hangover of the very early days, the beginning of earth, the emergence of men and women and their discovery of each other, described so quaintly in the Manugye. Wise men reviled, it was said, at the unions that to them seemed unbecoming, and the men and women "built houses, lived within enclosures, and following each other's example, secured a supply of food." The Burmese word for marriage, *ein-daung-pyu*, means 'set up house'; the throwing of stones that was done in the very early days as a mark of society's displeasure, the fee that was offered by the man and woman in partial atonement, are now parts of a joyous, frolicsome occasion.

The Manugye classes marriage in three kinds: that effected by parents of both parties; that contracted through a go-between, and marriage by mutual consent. This classification has no real validity today, though its value is in its reflection of the early social customs. Then the parents looked round for prospective daughters-in-law and the go-betweens helped in the search or to forge the golden links between the families after suitable prospects had been found; consent of the parents on both sides, and, of course, the prospective brides and grooms, would clinch the arrangements. The flow of gifts was not a one-way traffic, there was no rigid requirement of dowry, though parents on both sides would give what they could, often announcing the gifts at the ceremony, if there was one, or a meeting of the elders.

[1] Mi Mi Khaing, "People of the Golden Land"; also see a good description of "Marriages in Modern Burma" by Thaung Blackmore in *Eastern Horizon*, Honkong, April, 1961.

Certain requirements are prescribed by custom for a valid marriage. The parties must be capable as regards age and mind. The Dhammathats do not fix the age of competence for marriage, though they suggest that parents should give their sons and daughters in marriage when they reach the age of 15 or 16. It is generally accepted that a boy attains competence with puberty, and a girl when she reaches the age of 20 before which she needs parental consent. Consent of the parents may be presumed if a girl below 20 elopes, and they do nothing to reclaim her, though the right to reclaim, according to the Dhammathats, is not extinguished even though "she may have borne him ten children." In actual fact, however, it has been judicially settled that the right may not be kept alive so long, and consent may be implied from the conduct of the parents, as for example, in the case of a minor girl who has eloped and "subsequently returns to the village and lives with the man, and has children by him, openly and to the knowledge of her parents or guardians, and they do not enforce their rights of reclaiming the girl and separating her from the man without unreasonable delay..." The implied consent would then date back to the elopement and "convert the connection into a valid marriage." The children would also be legitimate.[1]

Another requisite is that the parties must be outside certain degrees of kindred or affinity. The Dhammathats do not define those degrees, though Major Spark's Code has a table of them without, as Jardine pointed out, any supporting authority. The kings enjoyed great laxity in this regard on the excuse that dynastic purity needed to be preserved. "No reigning family lasted three centuries or retained its vigour for more than three generations. One reason is the large-scale harem system which convention fastened on the monarch. Great kings did not transmit their character but shattered the mould, producing quantity at the expense of quality."[2] Outside of royalty, certain proprieties were observed, though there was no clear rule to determine propriety. "Thus, the union of uncle and niece, nephew and aunt, half-brother and half-sister, was permitted... and marriage with a deceased wife's sister – almost in all cases a younger sister – is considered most proper, the chief reason being that the children will not be given a stranger as step-mother. As regards cousins, generally speaking, union with agnates is strongly deprecated, while that with other cognates is not

[1] *Ma E Sein vs. Maung Hla Min*, 3 Ran. 455 F. B.; also the part on Burmese law in R. Lingat, *Les Régimes Matrimoniaux du Sud-Est de l'Asie*, translated from the French by Prof. Alan Gledhill.

[2] Harvey, *History of Burma*, p. 210.

looked upon with disfavour, provided the woman is on the same line as the man or below it. No case has arisen in which the validity of a marriage has been questioned on the ground of consanguinity or affinity, and, when one does, a considerable body of evidence will have to be led to prove prevailing customs."[1]

For a woman to enter into a valid marriage, she must not have a subsisting marriage tie. A widow or a divorcee can marry, and indeed such a woman, being emancipated from parental control by a previous marriage, does not need parental consent even if she should be below the age of 20, when she marries again. This requirement, however, does not apply to men, for polygamy is permitted by the customary law. "That there is a custom of polygamy among Burman Buddhists is beyond dispute," observed the Privy Council, "and that it is sanctioned by the Dhammathats is also beyond dispute. In view of existing custom, we think it is now too late to dissect the Dhammathats and to say that the law, as contained in certain portions of them, is not to be applied to Buddhists because it appears to have a Hindu origin and to have special reference to Hindu usages."[2] Polygamy, however, is not a popular institution. "It is legal, but except among officials and the wealthy, is seldom practised. In ordinary life a man with more than one wife is talked of as not being a very respectable person. This seems also to have struck the early European travellers in Burma, for we find many of them, like Nicolo Conti in 1430, remarking 'This people take only one wife'."[3]

The most important element of the Burmese Buddhist marriage, which is commonly described as a "consensual contract," is consent. The consent of the parents or the guardian is needed, as we have seen, if a girl is below the age of 20 and not yet emancipated. Time has weakened the parental power and control however, and today it is settled law and custom that the vital consent on which a marriage must be founded is that of the parties themselves. No longer can a father give away an unwilling minor daughter into marriage. Mutual consent of the parties, freely given, by tests laid down in section 14 of the Contract Act, and where the parties are of sound mind as tested by section 12 of the Act, is the indispensable ingredient.

[1] May Oung, *Leading Cases*, I, p. 5; Major Sparks makes this general statement: "The degrees of consanguinity and affinity are the same as under the English Canon Law, except in the case of a wife's sister and a brother's widow, marriage with whom is permitted by Burmese law."
[2] *Ma Wun Di vs. Ma Kin*, 4 LBR 175 P. C.
[3] C. J. F. S. Forbes, *Burma and Its People*, London, 1878, p. 64.

Consent of the parties to marry, their intention to enter the status of husband and wife, are the large factors in a marriage, proof of which therefore turns on conduct showing the consent and the intention. "My own personal view," remarked Baguley, J., in a case, "for what it may be worth, based on more than 20 years experience as a judicial officer, is that a marriage between Burmese Buddhists is created by cohabitation coupled with intent to become husband and wife. The ceremony is merely a way of publishing to all the world that the cohabitation, which is intended to follow it, is with the intention of creating a marriage tie between the couple. The ceremony is evidence of the intent, and is not a means of creating the tie in itself, in this way differing from the ceremony which actually brings into existence the marriage tie among Christians, Hindus and Mohammedans."[1] Cohabitation means living in conjugal relationship, not a clandestine arrangement. There must be an open avowal of the married status, going together to the pagoda and the monastery – of which romantic Burmese songs sing so fondly – and "eating together in public" being conduct of such nature. Conduct must lead friends, neighbours and relatives, to accept the parties as husband and wife, not merely feed them with food for gossip.[2] "Admission of status, joint visits to places of worship, joint acts of charity, the treatment accorded to the man by the woman's parents and relatives, and that accorded to the woman by the parents and relatives of the man, the character and position of the woman and her parents, and acting jointly in making or taking conveyances of property are relevant facts to consider."[3] Where there is a dispute, and proof of marital status has to depend only on habit and repute, then the facts have to be carefully examined, and a bare statement by a witness that the couple are husband and wife is held insufficient.[4] "Doubtless the laws which dispense with ceremony and registration leave the door open for uncertainty, mistake, and fraud," Jardine noted, "but in this respect other civilized nations have to encounter the same evils, and the only remedy is by legislation."[5] It has become popular and fashionable with the young people these days to go to a judge or magistrate and sign affidavits, in the presence of a few friends and elders,stating their competence and intention to marry. The affidavit

[1] *Ma Hla Me vs. Maung Hla Baw*, 7 Ran. 425.
[2] *Maung Maung vs. Ma Sein Kyi*, 1940 RLR 562; *Ma E Mai vs. Ma Kyi Kyi*, 1948 BLR 625.
[3] *Ma Wun Di vs. Ma Kin*.
[4] *U Tun Yin vs. Maung Ba Han*, 1949 BLR 443, H. C.
[5] Jardine, *Notes*, I, p. 5.

is then kept by the parties, the young man keeping the young woman's and vice versa, as 'certificate' of marriage and proof. This procedure saves the expense of big ceremonies and receptions, is quicker, and looks more 'legal' in that there are documents to keep which bear stamps and seals and signatures.[1]

One element of a valid marriage over which some doubt has been cast is consummation. In *Ma Hla Me vs. Maung Hla Baw* before the High Court, a suit in which the 'husband' sued for restitution of conjugal rights on the ground that a marriage ceremony had been performed and he had lived with his 'wife' in the home of her parents until he was driven out and denied access to her, the defence was successfully put up that there was in fact no consummation, and therefore no valid marriage. A search for reliable authority on the question was made, only to discover the great dearth. An earlier case, in which the validity of a marriage was in issue, was referred to, but it was found that there the parties not only performed a ceremony but, as if to make things doubly sure, had eloped before, and lived together in the same house after, and there was no difficulty in finding that marriage was established. In rejecting the petition for restoration of conjugal rights by holding the marriage unconsummated, and thus invalid, the Judge held that the "living together" that constituted evidence of a Burmese marriage meant more than "living together in the same house" but was a "refined equivalent for cohabitation." Neither the customs of Burmese society today, nor the Dhammathats where they do touch on the subject, though lightly, seem to fully support the decision.[2]

2. CONFLICTS OF LAW

The ordinary courts, and not ecclesiastical courts or special family courts, determine questions of Burmese customary law of the family. There is, therefore, no problem of parallel systems of courts competing for jurisdiction. Conflicts have, however, occurred in the choice of law, between Burmese customary law and the British codes, for example, and between 'Burmese Buddhist Law' and 'Chinese Buddhist Law'

[1] In my first experience in legal practice with a young couple who wanted me to draft a 'certificate' of marriage I did not know what to put in, and had to ask a clerk, did not know how much fee to charge, and as a small fee might make their great venture look small, charged 500 Burmese kyats ($. 100), stamped the documents with the largest seal I had, tied them up in ribbons of gold and red; the young couple went away happy, and, as far as my knowledge goes, remain so with their growing family.

[2] E Maung, *Burmese Buddhist Law*, Rangoon, 1937, pp. 20–26.

when the parties to a family dispute are 'Burmese Buddhists' and 'Chinese Buddhists'. Many of the conflicts, traceable on the one hand to the vague notion of 'personal law' and to the interpretation of s. 13 (1) of the Burma Laws Act on the other, have been resolved by judicial decision and legislation.

The notion of personal law is an ancient one. "The history of all laws open with an entirely personal conception of law: every man possessed only the rights and duties with which the laws of his own tribe, city, or class invested him, and could not be judged by any other."[1] From this arose the *professiones juris* or declarations of law which every one was obliged to make, when called upon, according to prescribed conditions. The rule that every person should be governed by his own laws had exceptions where a person's individual law could not be recognised and where the public interest ran counter to it. In the feudal period, when the life of wandering conquest had given place to a fixed home life, the principle of personality gave place to that of territoriality, and in each lord's domain, the local custom alone was applied. In Burma also the trend has been towards a uniform territorial law, and the presumption that 'Burmese Buddhist Law' applies in matters of the family to every person who professes Buddhism unless he can prove that his community practises other rules which have ripened into customary law.[2] The confusion that arose from the earlier notion of 'personal law' was further confounded by the separate systems of courts set up for 'Burma proper' and the hill areas. A Chin in the northern hills, for example, was governed not only by his local custom but by the Chin Hills Regulations for prescribed offences that he might commit, and the final appellate authority for him was the Governor who had personal responsibility for frontier areas affairs, and not the High Court.[3] With the abolition of the parallel systems of courts, the problem of their competition for jurisdiction has also disappeared to a large extent. The frontier areas – the 'backward tracts', the 'scheduled districts' and such – have now emerged as separate autonomous units of the Union of Burma and they have opted for a uniform legal system, while preserving their ancient customs inasmuch

[1] Josef Kohler, *Internationales Strafrecht*, 1917, quoted in Philip C. Jessup, *Transnational Law*, Yale, 1956, p. 41; Eggar, *Laws of India and Burma*, I, p. 28.

[2] A course on Burmese customary law, offered at the law faculty of the University of Rangoon, is still called Personal Law, though it is beginning to be better known as the Burmese Customary Law, indicating the general fading away of the personal law notion.

[3] *The King vs. Yoo Ngoon*, 1941 RLR 555; *Ma Thin vs. Maung Sei Tin*, 1949 BLR 74, S. C. (re. the Shan State judicial organization).

as they are suitable, as a necessary step in their cultural and social development.[1]

Mixed marriages between Burmese Buddhist women and non-Buddhist men, or the so-called 'Chinese Buddhists', gave rise to problems and inequities at first, and a long line of judicial decisions and special marriage laws form a bridge between the situation that appeared in the wake of British annexation, and the situation that prevails at the present day. "Since the passing of the country under British rule, large numbers of persons from other countries, chiefly India and China, have settled permanently in Burma. The indigenous races have no prejudices against alliances with forcigners and their religion offers no impediment to such. It was therefore inevitable that many of the settlers should have sought wives among the Burmese who, impelled by poverty, have consented to cohabit with them in the manner usual among their own people. In the eyes of their neighbours and friends they were lawfully wedded wives, and, except perhaps in the large towns, they preserve their independent habits and customs. It is only when questions of maintenance, divorce, or inheritance arise that they are suddenly confronted with the new law and they find themselves to be mere mistresses, their offspring bastards, both legal nonentities, except that the father may be compelled under the criminal law to maintain the latter. Many a case has come to light in which foreigners have lured young and ignorant Burmese women into what seemed to be a marriage and later, when it suited them to do so, repudiated the union on the strength of their own personal law. Why the personal law of one should be applied and that of the other utterly ignored does not seem to be clear."[2]

Judicial thinking seemed to have wandered astray at the start after imprecise definitions and names. Section 13 (1) of the Burma Laws Act spoke of 'Buddhist Law' but the common parlance for the customary law of the Burmese Buddhist family was Burmese Buddhist Law, which, by judicial logic, should not apply to Buddhists who were not Burmese. The notion of personal law also came into the thinking: Chinese from China, for example, were clothed in their own Chinese customary law, and if a Chinese man 'married' a Burmese Buddhist woman in Burma, and when their status came under question, claimed

[1] The constitution assigns the administration of justice and the organization of all courts subordinate to the High Court in the constituent units of the Union to the 'State Legislative List'. The States may, however, opt for a uniform system, pooling resources, and this is the purpose of The States Courts Act, 1953.

[2] May Oung, *Leading Cases*, I, p. 14.

to be governed by his own personal law, then his claim must be allowed despite the hardship it might cause the Burmese woman, despite the fact that he too was a Buddhist. "We all know," Jardine observed in an early case in which this thinking prevailed, "that the Courts apply different systems of both Hindu and Mohammedan law to people belonging to different races, countries or sects. I doubt, therefore, whether it is obligatory on our Courts here to apply the Burma Buddhist law to Buddhists from Ceylon or China. The subject teems with difficulties."[1] The notion of personal law was carried in one case to the extent of denying a Burmese Buddhist woman the maintenance provided for by section 488 of the Criminal Procedure Code, on the ground that the man was a Chinese Confucian and therefore the law applicable was Chinese customary law. "This case is typical," the Judge observed, "of the deplorable position of the women of Burma."[2]

Judges, however, soon paused to ponder, and began to wonder whether they had not permitted their minds to be too narrowly confined within the walls of words. If a 'marriage' had been contracted in Burma by Burmese custom, should not Burmese customary law be the guide in the settlement of questions arising out of the 'marriage'? Must the Courts go wildly searching for the proper law and its substance merely because a man in a marital dispute happened to have been born in some obscure village in China, or born and brought up in Burma but with a mixture of Chinese blood in his veins? Would it not be commonsense as well as sound social policy to go by the customary law of the society in which the marriage was contracted and the married lives were lived? The Judges who had been diligently studying Chinese customary law now began to consult commonsense and discovered that the commonsense view was also supported by conflicts of law decisions. In a case, thus, in which a man, born in Burma of a Chinese father and a Burmese mother, was involved, the Chief Court of Lower Burma held, after citing British cases in which it had the *lex loci contractus* determined the validity of marriages, that "there is no strong reason why the customary law of the man should be applied, and that of the woman utterly disregarded, at any rate up to and at the time of the marriage": the rule of *lex loci contractus* was permitted to weigh.[3]

The trend of judicial thinking culminated in *Ma Yin Mya vs. Tan*

[1] Hongku vs. Ma Thin, SJLB, p. 135; Hla Aung, "Sino-Burmese Marriages and Conflicts of Laws," *The Burma Law Institute Journal*, Rangoon, 1958.

[2] *Ma U vs. Maung Kyin Htat*, 4 *Burma Law Journal*, 1925, p. 255.

[3] *Sein Kyi vs. Ma E*, 8 LBR 399.

Yauk Pu in which a Full Bench of the High Court gave its ruling on the question referred: "In the case of Chinese Buddhists, is the Burmese Buddhist Law regarding marriage applicable to them as the *lex loci contractus* or, if not, which is the law applicable?" The answer, a unanimous affirmative, also laid down that a Chinese Buddhist must, if he wanted to escape from the application of Burmese Buddhist law prove that he was subject to a custom having the force of law in Burma, that the custom was opposed to the provisions of Burmese law applicable to the case, and that the application of the custom would not work injustice to the Burmese Buddhist woman in the case. The following comments of Rutledge, C.J., in which the development of Burmese law is reviewed, and the purpose of law in society put under focus, merit reproduction.

"The question (of which law applies in mixed marriages) has become acute in Burma by reason of the large number of Chinamen who marry Burmese women. Both belong to the great Mongolian branch of the human race, and have many points in common. But while by reason of a long conservative civilization the Chinese until recently were governed by legal customs which had crystallized several thousand years ago, the Burmans were subjected to a law which altered from time to time to meet the changed circumstances of the Burmese people, with the result that in matters of inheritance and property there is no country where the principle of equality of the sexes has been carried further than in Burma, and in regard to marriage where the marriage contract and status rest on consent alone and both parties to the marriage are equal partners. The effect of our Courts applying Chinese customary law to a Chino-Burmese marriage is to deprive a Burmese woman of practically all rights and in most cases brand her children as illegitimate. China has for a good many years been in a state of revolution. But when order and unity are once more established I do not think that any publicist would prophesy that the ancient customs which used to govern inheritance and marriage among the Chinese will be re-established. Again it must not be lost sight of that Chinamen have come and settled in Burma in growing numbers since the first occupation of the country. And more than any other race they have inter-married and joined in the social and religious life of the people of the country, so that the third generation so far as blood and manner of life are concerned are much more Burman than Chinese. To apply without enquiry the ancient customary law of China to these people seems to be unwise and impolitic unless we are forced to do so of necessity. In my opinion, not only are we not forced to do so, but the principles of private international law and the words of the Burma Laws Act forbid us to do so."[1]

Mugs from Chittagong, the Chin people, and the Shans who are resident in Burma and profess Buddhism are governed by Burmese customary law – as it is generally known – in their family relations, and the burden is on them to prove that that law is inapplicable.[2] While this principle became well settled after the decision in the *Ma Yin Mya* case it was held to test the validity and existence only of marriage, and the question of what law applied to inheritance and succession to the estate of a Chinese Buddhist, born in China but who established his domicile and died in Burma, was considered to be open. The opinion of the Full Bench of the High Court in *Phan Tiyok vs. Lim Kyin Kauk* was that Chinese customary law, and not Burmese Buddhist law, was the dominant law, and this thinking endured, though in increasingly diluted form, until the Privy Council decided that in inheritance and succession, even as in the form and validity of marriage, the Buddhist law of Burma must apply, the burden of proof resting on the person who asserts variance to prove that his personal laws vary. "The law which is described as 'the Buddhist law' in the statute," the Privy Council observed, "is like the Hindu and Mahomedan law intended to be applied by the Court as a law known to the Court, and administered by the Court of its own skill and competence... It cannot be confounded or identified with a foreign law which has to be proved as a matter of fact in each case by the appropriate evidence."[3] The Supreme Court in re-affirming the principle that "a Buddhist in Burma, irrespective of what his nationality is, and of whence he came, is governed by the Burmese Buddhist Law," further argued that the use of the definite article 'the' before 'Buddhist Law' in section 13 (1) of the Burma Laws Act clearly indicated the intention of the Legislature. "The object is that the Courts should apply only such Hindu Law to the Hindus, such Mohammedan Law to the Mohammedans, and such Buddhist Law to the Buddhists as is well known to the Courts and to the people in the country in the matter of marriage, inheritance, succession, etc. The Legislature never intended that the Courts should go roving about all over the world in search of law that would be applicable to parties in proceedings before them. But that is exactly what the learned Judges

[1] 5 Ran. 406.

[2] 1894 UBR 608; 1 Ran. 343.

[3] *Phan Tiyok vs. Lim Kyin Kauk* 8 Ran. 57, F. B.; also see *Tan Ma Shwe Zin vs. Tan Ma Ngwe Zin*, 10 Ran. 97; *Tan Ma She Zin vs. Koo Soo Chong*, 1939 RLR 548 P. C.

who applied Chinese customary law to the Chinese Buddhist in Burma did."[1]

To discover what the Burmese customary law is on a specific problem of the family is not, in theory at least, too difficult. It is local law for the courts, and access to the texts, the rulings, and the repositories of custom – whatever and wherever they may be – is open. Difficulties arise, however, when the courts have to ascertain, for example, what Hindu law is that applies to the Hindu immigrants. Here, the problem is not one of choice of law, but the discovery of its relevant substance. Is the law that which applies between the Hindu communities in India from which the immigrants have come? But then the immigrants, some of whom are three or four generations removed from the original Hindu immigrants, may well have developed their own customs which are but a faint echo of the customs that live in the communities in India. The Courts seemed at first to have inclined towards looking to India as the primary source of the Hindu law that could be applied to problems of Hindu families in Burma, even as they had looked to China to supply the law to apply to problems of Sino-Burmese families in Burma. Thus, in a civil second appeal before the High Court in which the validity of a Hindu marriage was challenged and a Hindu girl reclaimed by her parents, the Court relied on Hindu Marriage Act, passed by Parliament in India in 1955, to rule that there was a valid marriage, and that under the new Act inter-caste marriages were no longer discountenanced. It was argued for the parents that the Act of 1955 was not "existing law" in Burma under s. 226 of the constitution and therefore had no force, but the Court ruled that the definition of existing law did not include personal law, and, after all "the Indian Legislature is a competent authority to pass Acts relating to Hindu Law and it is to the Indian Legislature that all Hindus must look for their protection in respect of cases coming within the sphere of their personal law."[2] A different view was held in a later case heard by a Bench of two Judges of the High Court. A Hindu resident in Rangoon was alleged to have committed a bigamous marriage in India, and this offence of bigamy – a new offence created by the Hindu Marriage Act, 1955, which, among other things, made polygamy illegal – was incidentally mentioned in a prosecution launched against him in the court of a Magistrate in Rangoon. Comments on the facts of the case appeared in a newspaper, against whom proceedings in contempt were started.

[1] *Daw Thike vs. Cyoung Ah Lin*, 1951 BLR 133 S. C.
[2] *Ramadhar Keot vs. Ratipal Ahir*, 1958 BLR 11, H. C. per Aung Khine, J.

The High Court decided that the contempt action could not lie, for the lower Court had taken cognizance of the charge of bigamy in error, and comments on the case could not therefore amount to contempt. The prohibition of polygamy by the Act passed in India had no force in Burma, the Court held, for it had not ripened into Hindu law applicable among the Hindus of Burma by long usage and custom. "The Hindu law as recognized by the Courts in Burma is the customary law relating to Hindus and the law laid down by the decision of the Courts. According to this law, a Hindu may marry again, though he has a wife living as Hindu law permits polygamy though it does not approve of the practice. In India an absolute prohibition against polygamy was enacted by s. 17 of the Hindu Marriage Act. This being a statute law enacted by the Indian Legislature it could not per se have any effect on the Hindus in Burma; it would only be recognized if after generations of obedience to the statute, new migrants from India come into Burma and claim that so far as they were concerned monogamy was a custom having the force of law for them."[1]

The trend, if not the established position, is to regard law as territorial, to be applied by the Courts as known to them, or as may be discovered from local custom, for the benefit of the society in which the law functions. The notion of personal law, that clings to the wandering people wherever they may go, has faded. The niceties of legal definitions have been overcome, and judicial thinking seems to have broken free from the narrow confinement of words and punctuation marks, to strive for the real purpose and function of law in society. The eternal problem remains, however, of defining that purpose and function in harmony with society's goals and values. Once the purpose and function become sharp and clear the striving for their achievement becomes simpler.

The attitude of the Courts that it is the known laws and customs of the society which they serve that they must apply, and with the main purpose of promoting the best interests of that society, goes beyond the province of family law. A case in point arose over the problem of dual nationality. The constitution, and the citizenship laws of Burma, recognize only one citizenship to the exclusion of others. The People's Republic of China, sprawled heavily beyond Burma's northern borders, claims all overseas Chinese – people with Chinese blood in

[1] *Union* of *Burma vs. M.V. Gadhia*, Cr. Misc. Appln. 18, 1960, February 1, 1961; V. Fitzgerald, "Indian and Far Eastern Cases on the Conflict of Laws," 16 *Journal of Comparative Legislation and International Law* (1934).

their veins, even if only a few drops – as its citizens with rights and responsibilities. By this new fundamental law of the People's Republic, Chinese in Burma who have been born and brought up in the country and are natural-born citizens as well as thousands of Burmese who have a small dilution of Chinese blood in them, all become Chinese citizens in the eyes of Peking. The force of the fundamental law of Peking was tested in Rangoon in an election petition in which a losing candidate for Parliament tried to nullify the victory of his opponent on the ground that the latter had some Chinese blood in him, and by Peking's law he was Chinese, and therefore ineligible by Burma's law to take his seat in Parliament. The Election Petitions Tribunal had no difficulty in rejecting the petition. The respondent, it was held, was a Burmese citizen and he had not been deprived of his citizenship by any law that Peking might choose to make. The governing law, the Tribunal decided, was the law of Burma, and the Tribunal was "by no means conversant with the law and practice prevailing in the Republic of China as regards questions of Chinese nationality and no evidence whatsoever has been led to enlighten us on this point."[1]

In the early days of British rule when the legal system was being 'modernised' with the import of the codes from India and of the principles of the common law, questions in the nature of conflict occasionally arose in the determination of the scope of Burmese customary law. One question was whether a suit founded on a breach of promise to marry must be decided by the customary law, or by the Contract Act. Judicial opinion seemed to favour customary law as the proper law, and a Full Bench of the Chief Court of Lower Burma held that as every marriage must be preceded by an offer and its acceptance, the prior agreement to marry formed an integral part of every marriage and any question arising from the promise must be deemed as one regarding marriage, and within the ambit of Burmese customary law.[2] A Full Bench of the High Court later drew a distinction between an agreement *in presenti*, contemporaneous with cohabitation and forming an integral part of the marriage, which would be governed by the customary law, and an agreement to marry *in futuro* which would neither affect the status of the parties nor form an integral part of the proposed marriage, to which the Contract Act and the "general law of the land" would apply. The case was one in which a young Burmese boy of 15

[1] *U San Win vs. U Sin Koi*, election petition 22 of 1956, Tribunal's report in *Burma Gazette*, I, February 22, 1958.

[2] *Maung Gale vs. Ma Hla Yin*, 11 LBR 99 F. B.

had an affair with a Burmese girl of about the age, and when she was with child refused to marry her. The lower court to which a suit for damages for breach of promise was brought awarded a decree on the ground that the suit was governed by Burmese customary law in the eyes of which a boy of 15 was competent to marry – physical competence being the test – and therefore his promise, or implied promise, to marry could form a cause of action. If, however, as the appellate court thought, the subject matter was not one relative to marriage, but that of contract, to be governed by the Contract Act which then would test competence by the Majority Act, then the boy being under 18 would not be competent to contract without the support of his parents' consent, and a suit for breach of contract would not therefore lie. It was on a reference from the appellate court that the High Court gave its Full Bench decision distinguishing between matters of marriage, to which the customary law applies, and contracts which stand apart from marriage though they may be its prelude.[1]

Thus, gradually, the scope of Burmese customary law came to be defined by judicial decision. Where there were gaps in it they were filled by legislation, as, for example, in the matter of guardianship of minor children where the parents are living apart by the Guardian and Wards Act.[2] Legislation may supercede customary law where that law is considered obsolete, or strengthen it where it is considered inadequate.

3. SPECIAL MARRIAGE ACTS

There have been suggestions that Burmese customary law should be codified, and attempts have been made in that direction in a few subjects which are considered to be ripe for the treatment. The Codification Committee which worked for a few years from 1924, and the Committee on Buddhist Wills, appointed in 1938, were recent examples.[3] The consensus of opinion has, however, been that the customary law has attained maturity to grow naturally by itself without the aid of legislation, that its broad principles are known well enough and that reduced to cold print they will only become hard and rigid and lose

[1] *Maung Tun Aung vs. Ma Aye Kyi*, 14 Ran. 215 F. B.

[2] *Ma Thein Me vs. Maung Po Gywe*, 8 BLT 73.

[3] Sir Guy Rutlege, C. J., was chairman of the codification committee, and U E Maung and U Thein Maung were among the members; U E Maung served as secretary of the committee on Buddhist wills.

much of their living quality. The contrary view is that the "mass of case-law, along with a few fragmentary statutes, some ill-understood books, many of which have either never been closely and comparatively studied, or have been subjected to such a process only recently and with no certainty that unsatisfactory materials from the results will weigh heavily in Courts, and in default of these unsatisfactory materials from evidence of custom, which may seldom be agreed, and even if agreed may not lead to reliable or consistent inferences" only create a "happy hunting ground for the lawyer."[1] The truth seems to lie in-between: the situation is not as bad as it may look, though certainly it is not as tidy as it may be made by a compact little code; nor is the situation one that justifies the complacency of those who consider that laws and customs grow naturally and reveal themselves to those who are blessed with special wisdom.

Though the Burmese customary law of the family as such has not be codified, a few statutes have been made to supplement it where the need is felt. The protection of Burmese Buddhist women who enter into unions with non-Buddhists resident in the country is a subject that has called for legislation on considerations of policy. Early legislation merely provided the forms and procedures by which valid marriages might be contracted between persons who professed the Buddhist faith, and those who did not; Buddhist women who availed themselves of the provisions of the Acts received the status of wife, their children legitimacy, even though the marriage and the family came under statutory laws other than the Burmese customary law. The Special Marriage Act, 1872, the first in a series of such Acts, required that neither party must, at the time or the marriage, have a husband or a wife living; the man must be 18 years old at least, and the woman at least 14; if below 21, each party must also have the consent of the parents or guardian; the parties must not be related in any degree of consanguinity or affinity according to any law to which either of them was subject. Due notice of intention to marry must be filed with the Registrar of the district, and in the absence of objections, the marriage could be solemnized with the parties and three witnesses signing a declaration in the presence of the Registrar. A marriage contracted under the Act must be monogamous, whatever the religion of the man or the woman might be, and if he or she belonged to an undivided family by the law or custom of his or her religion the marriage severed that

[1] J. D. M. Derrett, "The Codification of Personal Law in India," *Indian Yearbook of International Affairs*, Madras, 1957.

family tie. Matters of divorce came under the Divorce Act, of succession under the Succession Act. The Buddhist man or woman who married under the Act lost the right to adopt.

The Act of 1872 was amended and somewhat enlarged in scope by an amending Act of 1923, making it possible for Buddhists and non-Buddhists to marry, but such marriages took the families outside the pale of Burmese customary law, and disadvantages for Buddhist women still remained. The Buddhist Women's Special Marriage and Succession Act which came into force on the 1st. April, 1940, shortly before war came to Burma, was designed specially for the protection of Buddhist women's rights when they contracted marriages with non-Buddhist men.[1] In moving that the bill be referred to a Select Committee for study and report, a member of the House of Representatives pointed out that the need for the law had arisen largely from the wrong notion of personal law. "As long as the parties to whom a particular form of personal law applies are of the same community, we find that there is nothing unsatisfactory, and no hardship is caused... but we find that the Courts in Burma have allowed the personal laws of the foreigners to override the personal law of the natives, the personal laws of the male foreigner to override the personal laws of the Buddhist woman... and much injustice is done... We should make our law territorial, that means, a law which will be applicable to each and every person resident in Burma."[2]

The Act sought to bring into the operation of Burmese customary law all marriages – and the families they created – in which the women were Buddhists "belonging to any of the indigenous races of Burma" and the men were non-Buddhists, and thereby to make Burmese customary law territorial and not personal. The requirements for a valid marriage were that the parties were of sound mind; the man must not be less than 18, nor the woman less than 16 years old; in the case of a party below 20 the express consent of the father or mother or the guardian must be obtained; in the case of the woman, she must not have a subsisting marriage. Fourteen days' notice of intention to marry must be given to the Registrar of Marriages – and, for the sake of convenience, all village headmen were named Registrars – and at the end of the period the marriage would be solemnized, in the absence of valid objection, and recorded in the register. A Buddhist woman or

[1] The Special Marriage Act, India Act 3 of 1872; Amendment, Act 30 of 1923; Buddhist Women's Special Marriage and Succession Act, Burma Act 24 of 1939.

[2] U Tha Saing in House of Representatives, *Proceedings*, III, 9, p. 553, Rangoon, 1938.

her parent, guardian, brother or sister, could give information to a Registrar of the district in which she was resident that she had been cohabiting with a non-Buddhist without being legally married to him, and the Registrar must then summon the parties, explain that they could legalize their union under the Act, and proceed to do so if they agreed. If one party was willing but the other was not, the Registrar must advise the willing party that a suit for breach of promise to marry, or for seduction, might be resorted to.

The family launched under the Act came under Burmese customary law in questions of divorce, inheritance and succession, and ownership of properties. If the husband was a Hindu, Sikh or Jain, and belonged to an undivided family, his rights in that family devolved on the wife and children if he died before partition of property in that family. Any child born of the couple before the marriage was solemnized under the Act was deemed to have been born in lawful wedlock. The Act did not extinguish the right of adoption of either party, nor the privilege of the man to have more than one lawful wife under his own law and custom.

War and military occupation prevented the Act from coming into full play in Burma, and a new Act was drafted and passed in the Burmese language by Parliament in 1954. Certain improvements were also introduced into the Act to provide for the better interests of the Buddhist woman. The age of competence for the non-Buddhist male is no longer fixed: if he is physically competent, he comes within the ambit of the new law. The woman's age of competence is also lowered from 16 to 14, though the need for parental consent is maintained if she is below 20. If a non-Buddhist man and a Buddhist woman live together in such manners as would raise the presumption that they are man and wife by Burmese custom – had they both been Buddhists – the new Act establishes the presumption that they are lawfully married from the time they started to live together. The couple might formalize the marriage by applying to the Registrar to enter it in the records. A marriage performed under the Act or presumed by it, is governed by Burmese customary law. If the husband, whose law and custom prohibits a legal marriage with a Buddhist woman, divorces her or seeks to nullify the union, he must leave her his share of the joint property and the custody of all the children, whom he must support through their years of minority; the wife is also entitled to compensation. If a woman who is a citizen of Burma becomes a convert to Buddhism during the subsistence of a marriage, then the family comes under Burmese customary law, and if the husband divorces her on the ground that his customary law prohibits a legal marriage with a Buddhist woman, he must maintain her in standards of life to which she has become accustomed before her conversion to the Buddhist faith, and she is entitled to keep her separate property, and the children whom the man must maintain in their minority. The expression "Buddhist woman" is also given a wider scope than that of the earlier Act. Now a Buddhist woman is a citizen of Burma who professes the Buddhist faith, or a citizen both of whose parents are Buddhist.[1]

4. DIVORCE

The Special Marriage Acts of 1872 and 1923, as noticed earlier, provide for marriages between persons who profess various religious faiths such as Buddhism, the Hindu, Islam, Jaina, Sikh, etc., and legalizes such unions which would otherwise be of doubtful validity. When one party is a Christian the marriage may be performed under the Christian Marriage Act, either in a religious ceremony or at the Registrar's office without one. These marriages are special marriages which fall outside Burmese customary law and are governed, in questions of divorce, by the Divorce Act. If a Buddhist man or a woman embraces the religion of Islam, for example, and goes through a marriage with another party of that faith, the marriage comes under the law of Islam, or Muhammedan law as recognized by the Burma Laws Act, which would also be the law governing matters of divorce. With those marriages which are removed from the province of Burmese customary law we are not concerned in this study.

There are several grounds for divorce in Burmese law, most of which are universal: e.g. cruelty, desertion, adultery. One special feature of the Burmese family in this matter, however, is that mutual consent can bring the marriage to an end. Just as a man and a woman can come together, set up home as husband and wife and establish their status as such, without any ceremony or entertainment of friends, without resort to the courts or the administrative authorities, so they can end the marriage. As it is usual at a bethrothal or a marriage to invite the elders of the village or the neighbourhood, the relatives and friends, and offer them food and pickled tea and tender information on what is about to happen, so it is usual when husband and wife decide to part

[1] The Buddhist Women's Special Marriage and Succession Act, No. 32 of 1954.

to report to the elders, the relatives and the friends. Some publicity conscious people announce their divorce in the newspapers, and it is not uncommon for a husband to proclaim that his wife of yesterday is no longer his wife today, and he is not responsible for any debts she may contract, etc., and for the wife to proclaim in rebuttal that she is not divorced, and remains what she has been, and the marriage tie is very much intact. Often, after the proclamations have been made in the newspapers for several weeks, to the delight of social gossip and the advertising managers of the newspapers, the couples come together again and all goes on as before.

"With this facility for divorce," observed Fielding Hall from his experience as an administrator in upper Burma, "it is remarkable how uncommon it is. In the villages and amongst respectable Burmans in all classes of life it is a great exception to divorce or be divorced. The only class amongst whom it is at all common is the class of hangers-on to our administration, the clerks and policemen, and so on. It is terrible to see how demoralizing our contact is to all sorts and conditions of men... I have even tried to find out in small villages what the number of divorces were in a year, and tried to estimate from this percentage. I made it from 2 to 5 per cent of the marriages, but I cannot offer these figures as correct for any large area... The facility for divorce has other effects too. It makes a man and a woman very careful in their behaviour to each other. The chain that binds them is a chain of mutual forbearance, of mutual endurance, of mutual love; and if these be broken, then is the bond gone. Marriage is no fetter about a man or woman, binding both to that which they may get to hate."[1] Another British administrator found that in Burmese society "the legal marriage tie is easily formed, and as easily dissolved. Openly living together as man and wife, and eating out of the same dish, is as perfect a form of marriage as a whole string of ceremonies before the village elders and signing an agreement to separate. Except in large towns, where there is a mixed population, prostitution and its frightful evils are unknown. Illegitimate children, at least those having that status, are by their easy marriage customs rare, and wives are as generally faithful as with us."[2]

The Burmese word for divorce is *kwa*, and for separation is *kwe*; these words are loosely used and interchanged and when it is said that a couple is *kwe-kwa* one does not know whether the husband and the wife are separated and divorced once and for always, or whether they

[1] *The Soul of a People*, pp. 218– 220.
[2] Forbes, *Burma and Its People*, pp. 64–65.

are apart by force of circumstance and longing to be together again. *Karma* or destiny is the governing force in Burmese life, and when the astrologers, after looking at the stars, say that the stars of the husband and the wife are not sailing along happily together but at angry cross purposes, then indeed there is the serious situation of *kan-ma-sat*, of destinies not linked together, and a temporary divorce, just to please the stars – or cheat them – may be called for. Such a temporary divorce, or in Burmese a *gyo-byenan-bye* divorce, is recognized by the Courts as just what it purports to be. Thus, in an early case, where the wife lay seriously ill, and the astrologers advised that a temporary severance was needed to get her star out of an eclipse, the husband gave her a document of divorce. The next day she died, and the question arose whether the divorce was real or temporary, and the Courts, with the High Court of Calcutta agreeing as the final court, held that it was a temporary divorce by recognized Burmese custom.[1] The plea of *kan-ma-sat* as a ground for a real, legal divorce, however, is not accepted unless there is proof of a serious matrimonial fault or offence which would on its own have been a valid ground for divorce. Otherwise "divorce at mere caprice" would become an institution, and "it would be open to a husband who had no joint property but merely his monthly earnings to avoid complying with maintenance orders by merely claiming a *kan-ma-sat* divorce and abandoning the non-existent or trifling joint property of his marriage."[2]

When serious matrimonial faults or offences are put forward as grounds for divorce, the parties either accept a settlement, under arbitration of elders and friends, for partition of property, and part. Or they may go to the courts for a decree. It was thought at one time that a suit for bare divorce did not lie unless the suit also asked for partition of property, but a Privy Council decision has settled that divorce and partition form two separate causes of action for two separate suits, if preferred, for though "the partition may no doubt be treated as relief consequential upon the divorce, and dealt with in the same suit, the evidence is different, and the ground for divorce must be first and separately proved as a distinct cause of action before any question of partition can properly arise."[3]

Desertion is a ground for divorce, if it is committed with the inten-

[1] *Maung Ba Oh vs. Maung San Bu*, Chan Toon's Leading Cases, I, p. 137, also cited in S. Roy, *Custom and Customary Law in India*, Tagore Law Lectures, Calcutta, 1911, p. 339.

[2] *Ma Hmon vs. Maung Tun Kauk*, 1 Ran. 722.

[3] *Maung Pe vs. Ma Lon Ma Gale*, 6 LBR 18, P. C.

tion to end the marriage tie, and persisted for prescribed periods of time. If it is the wife who leaves the husband, the period is one year, at the end of which the husband may, by "an express act of volition," terminate the marriage tie. If the husband deserts, the wife must wait for three years, at the end of which she may actively sever the tie, such as by marrying again. If the husband is away on a business trip, or to the wars, or on foreign study, then, of course, the intention to dissolve the marriage being absent, time does not run against the marriage, and she must wait. A husband who is compelled, against his wishes obviously, to serve a long term of imprisonment, is held not to have deserted his wife, and if she marries again while he is in jail, she is guilty of desertion herself, and adultery.[1]

"Any husband and wife living together," lays down the Manugye, "if the husband saying he does not wish her for a wife, shall have left the house, and for three years shall not have given her one leaf of vegetables or one stick of firewood, at the expiration of three years, let each have the right to take another wife and husband. If the wife not having affection for the husband, shall leave the house and where they were living together, and, if during one year he does not give her one leaf of vegetables or one stick of firewood, let each have the right of taking another husband or wife; they shall not claim each other as husband and wife; let them have the right to separate and marry again."[2] The rule laid down by Manugye in the matter of desertion has caused great debate over the decades and through the various Benches of the High Court, including the Full Bench, and through the Privy Council, on the question whether divorce is "automatic" at the end of the prescribed periods of desertion. Is "automatic divorce" – an attractive proposition in this age of automation – an integral part of the Burmese family life? The Judges spent a great deal of their considerable legal learning on the question, and as judges and lawyers do everywhere, they came up with brilliant arguments and weighty authorities in support of the affirmative answer.[3] They also came up with brilliant arguments and weighty autorities in support of the negative answer.[4] They overruled

[1] *Aung Byu vs. Thet Hnin*, 8 LBR 50.

[2] *Kinwunmingyi Digest*, II, p. 227.

[3] *Ma Nyun vs. Maung San Thein*, 5 Ran. 537 F. B.; *U Thein vs. Ma Khin Nyun*, 1948 BLR 108; in *Ma Saw Khin vs. Maung Tun Aung Gyaw*, 6 Ran. 79, the Privy Council did not decide the question of automatic dissolution of the marriage tie, but stressed that since the matter was serious a strict construction of the rules of the Dhammathats must be made, and both desertion and failure to maintain must be fully satisfied.

[4] *Thein Pe vs. U Pet*, 3 LBR 175, F. B.; in *U Pe vs. U Maung Maung Kha*, 10 Ran. 261, P. C., the Privy Council ruled that a wife did not, by merely deserting her husband, commit a fault causing her to forfeit her interest in the property of the marriage.

one another, differed, distinguished, dissented, but the scales steadily weighed against acceptance of automatic divorce. The Full Bench of the High Court has now decided that the marriage tie "is not dissolved without an act of volition on the part of the deserted spouse showing his or her intention to determine the marriage relation or without conduct revealing a desire for divorce on the part of the deserted party." In the case, in which a wife sued her husband from whom she was separated for maintenance for herself and their child, it was held that he could not be deemed to have deserted her from the date of the institution of the suit, and if at the end of the prescribed period of time he could argue that the marriage had been dissolved automatically, it would amount to divorce by mere caprice – which is not permitted by Burmese law – and to reward a man for his acts of default. The Supreme Court has confirmed the decision and pointed out that desertion by the husband only "evidences his desire for dissolution of the marriage bond, and cannot in itself suffice to dissolve the bond created by mutual consent of the husband and wife. For that bond to be dissolved, it is necessary that the wife reciprocates the desire, and the reciprocation may be express or by conduct clearly pointing in that direction."[1]

A man may enter the priesthood and leave the earthly life behind, and then, as it is said figuratively though not fully accurately, he "dies a civil death." His wife is freed from the marriage bond, and may remarry. If, on the other hand, the man enters the priesthood only for a short period, to meditate and seek solace, or to appease his stars, then the wife waits. A man may shave his head and put on the yellow robes of the Buddhist priest, taking the vow of celibacy and poverty, yet he may weaken, break his vow and return to the lay life and his family again. The wife often sees to it that he does. Thus a story is told of a man named Ko Hsin who found life in the village burdensome. Business was bad, he had hurt his foot, and since his wife Ma Paw had to go round selling vegetables he had to look after the children at home and boil the rice. "He thought it would be good to become a monk. Then he would not have to boil rice. He would be able to turn his eyes towards the Supreme Good. His wife and children would gain merit by him. He felt certain that the time for his release from the sorrows of rebirth was at hand. He would endeavour to become a small god." Thus he became a monk, promising his wife he would return in a month, but staying on. Ma Paw's aunt from another village came to help out

[1] *Daw Khin Pu vs. Dr. Tha Mya*, 1949 BLR 283, H. C., F. B.; *Dr. Tha Mya vs. Daw Khin Pu*, 1951 BLR 108, S. C.

in the home, but as time dragged by she grew tired, and said, "Tell your monk to cast off the robes. I cannot stay on longer as a servant in your house." Ma Paw, being woman, knew how to handle her man. She took the son to the monastery one morning in a bullock cart, herself dressed in fine clothes. "My Aunt wants to return to her village," she humbly reported to the Holy One, "and I shall be unable to look after the children and keep shop at the same time. That is why I beg permission of the Celibate to allow me and the two children to go live with my Aunt in her village. The eldest son will be left in the Celibate's care." She wiped away a tear from her downcast face and continued, "The Cilebate may continue to be a monk throughout his life if that is his wish. His humble lay woman will try to make a living somehow. The Celibate's world and hers are different worlds; there is a vast gap between them. Since she still has two children, if she can find someone to depend upon somewhere else, she desires to accept him. That is why she wishes to make things clear now so that complications may not arise later." The Celibate uttered a cry of amazement, and his hands which clutched the yellow robes trembled. "There are too many drunkards in your Aunt's village," the Holy One said at last showing real earthly concern, "I will return to the lay life."[1] Of such daily happenings in Burmese society neither the Dhammathats nor the judicial decisions have any record.

Cruelty is another ground for divorce. An isolated instance of ill-treatment or violence is not sufficient; there must be physical violence or infliction of mental pain with indifference to, or delight in, the pain caused to the sufferer.[2] Aggravated cruelty, such as the infliction of grievous hurt, may forfeit the guilty spouse of his or her share of the joint property on divorce, for the partition of property goes by the cause of the divorce and the guilt of the offending party.[3] The husband's adultery, unless accompanied also by cruelty to the wife, is no ground for a divorce.[4] If, however, the wife commits adultery, the husband may divorce her, or condone the offence.[5] The condonation may be express or implied, but repetition may revive the condoned offence.

[1] *A Treasury of Modern Asian Stories*, ed. Milton & Clifford, New York, 1961, see the story *His Spouse* by Zawgyi U Thein Han, translated by U Win Pe.

[2] *Maung Kywe vs. Ma Thein Tin*, 7 Ran. 790.

[3] *Daw Pu vs. Maung Tun Kya*, 1946 RLR 125.

[4] *Ma Thein Nwe vs. Maung Kha*, 7 Ran. 451, differing from the decision of the Chief Court of Lower Burma in *Maung Hme vs. Ma San*, 9 LBR 191 F. B., in which the husband's adultery was considered a good ground for the wife to sue for divorce as by mutual consent.

[5] *Ma Dun Mai vs. Maung San Tun*, AIR 1938 Ran. 168.

As polygamy is legal, the husband's taking another wife without the consent of the first wife may, only under certain circumstances, give ground to that wife for a divorce. The Dhammathats say that if the first wife is barren – "that is, if she does not conceive after eight years" – the husband may take another wife without her consent. This simple test of who is the barren one is also prescribed: "if the husband does not beget children with another wife, it cannot be said that his former wife is barren, for he it is who is unproductive. The property brought by him at the time of separation from the former wife shall now be restored to her." Other good causes for taking another wife are the wife's bearing daughters only, or her being afflicted with leprosy or a similar disease, her immodest conduct.[1] The Full Bench of the Chief Court of Lower Burma decided that if any of these grounds exists, the husband does not need the wife's consent in taking a second wife; in the absence of the ground, the wife, whose dignity is injured by the second marriage, may sue for divorce.[2] The case dealt with the wife's right to divorce her husband if he took a second wife without her consent, and no judicial decisions exist which would support the husband's right to divorce the first wife if she is barren, or only bears female children, etc., and it would appear that the rule in the Dhammathats that she may be "put away" on any of those grounds is obsolete and contrary to Burmese social custom in which while sons are cherished daughters also enjoy equal standing in the family.

5. RESTITUTION OF CONJUGAL RIGHTS

At one time when it was thought that divorce by mere caprice of either party was permissible in Burmese customary law, the question of restitution of conjugal rights was deemed irrelevant. If the husband wished to discard the wife, all he had to do was to give her the *Kobo* or "price of the body" as compensation, and perhaps other shares of the family property, and that would put an end to the marriage. Similarly if the wife wished to end the bond, all she needed to do was leave and surrender some shares of the property to which she would otherwise have been entitled as the faultless party. As judicial opinion turned against the notion of divorce by mere caprice, room was opened for suits for restitution of conjugal rights.

[1] *Kinwunmingyi Digest*, II, p. 191.
[2] *Maung Hme vs. Ma Sein*, 9 LBR 191, F. B.

Today, such suits lie. A suit must be founded on a subsisting marriage, and either the wife, or the husband, may file it. The plaintiff must prove absence of fault on his or her part, and that the defendent has withdrawn from cohabitation without justifiable cause.[1] Illtreatment or desertion by the plaintiff is a good defence to the suit. The minority of the wife is not a good defence, however, for marriage has emancipated her from parental control and given her the status of wife.[2] A wife may not sue for divorce on the ground that her husband has committed adultery, but this constitutes a good defence against his suit for restitution of conjugal rights.[3] A husband who is under a duty to maintain his wife may not evade the duty by way of a decree for restitution. If he wins such a decree he must abide by its conditions sincerely. Where a wife had left her husband because he brought a "lesser wife" to the house, and he sued for restitution and received a decree on condition that he provided a separate residence for the wife, the High Court held that an order for maintenance could stand if he failed to comply with the condition.[4]

[1] *Maung Sein vs. Khin Thet Gyi*, 2 UBR (1904–06), 5.
[2] *Maung Myat Tha vs. Ma Thon*, 2 UBR (1892–96) 200.
[3] *Ma Thein Nwe vs. Maung Kha*, 7 Ran. 451.
[4] *Maung Po Kwe vs. Ma Pwa Shein*, 1939 RLR 741.

CHAPTER FIVE

CHILDREN OF THE FAMILY

1. NATURAL CHILDREN

This chapter may well begin with a plea. It has long been said with pride in Burma that the family is so close knit by feelings of love and duty that the young grow up to be good citizens naturally and the old grow old gracefully, that there is nothing but beauty and happiness in family life, unmarred by juvenile crime, untroubled by angry young people, unembarrassed by old unwanted people tottering about on the fringes of bare subsistence. Burma is an abundant land, and in the early days when the population was small there was plenty for the people to eat and more than enough to give them their small needs in their contented lives. Burma has not grown bigger or richer, but the population has been shooting up from 16 million in 1940 to 21 million estimated in the sample census of 1953-54, and it hovers today over the 22 million mark. The per capita income, about .56 Burmese kyats or 10 U.S. cents per day, is among the lowest in the world.[1] In times when there are floods or failure of crops, as there were on tragic scales in 1961, starvation, an unfamiliar ghost, stalks the poorer areas of the country. Mothers were reported, in 1961, to have sold their infants for petty amounts of money, partly because they needed the money for themselves to live, partly because the infants needed homes which could give them food and life. Extreme poverty shatters the family, and neither law nor custom can hold it together then. Great efforts need to be marshalled in the building of the economy, in the education of the young, in giving them hope and greater horizons, in raising them right, in gently correcting them when they err.

Little, for example, has been done to prevent, or cure, juvenile delinquency. A committee was appointed in 1927, the Government acknowledging that "in spite of the generous qualities of its people, this Province is unfortunately not free from the responsibility for unfortunate children growing up in circumstances which warp or pervert their minds and lead them directly into a life of crime, and mainly owing to financial considerations the Government has not yet been able, by adopting the best modern precedents to its needs to ensure

[1] Chamber of Deputies, *Proceedings*, II, 1, p. 4, August 30, 1956.

that children and young persons falling into crime shall be given the best opportunity of reforming and growing up into honest and useful citizens."[1] The committee recommended several measures, such as the expansion of reformatory school system, the improvement of aftercare and rehabilitation, the opening of boys clubs and homes, the institution of juvenile and family courts. Few of the recommendations were carried into effect with any zeal, though they were all highly appreciated and accepted "in principle" and the members of the committee warmly thanked for the invaluable services they had rendered, etc. etc. The Young Offenders Act, passed into law in 1930, was one concrete result of the committee's work, but the problem was larger than a law or the Government alone could handle, and social conscience has remained untroubled by its increasing size and seriousness. Buddhism which sees in every human being a potential Buddha, did not concern itself with social problems, for there is the law of karma which controls the wheel of life, and each individual must go the destined way, and to the best of his ability build the destiny for his next existence. In many ways, though not in all, the religion regards indifference as a virtue, and indifference does not make a potent stirrer-up of the social conscience. People who would give all their savings to a religious festival, towards the building of a pagoda, or covering the images at the temples with gold leaves, go about unmoved when unfortunate children wander in search of homes, or go waste in need of schooling. The tradition of sending the young boys to the monastery for an elementary education – a tradition which is accredited with having raised the quality and rates of literacy in the country – is slowly dropping off, as society changes, old values replaced by the new, or just fading away without replacement. Much needs to be done to conserve and nurture the young. Much needs to be done to control the population growth – which has been rapid, though the stage of "explosion" seems to be some way away yet – and talks by Burmese leaders in responsible positions, who should know better, that the population needs to be doubled are less than intelligent. More needs to be done through voluntary work at all levels to help the young build character, body and mind, and find meaning and purpose in life. Laws are not sufficient in themselves; courts without the inspiration can only be empty gestures.[2]

[1] *Report* of the Committee appointed to consider the treatment of Juvenile Delinquency in Burma, Rangoon, 1928.

[2] A more elaborate Act for the protection of Children was passed in 1955, superceding some of the sections of the Young Offenders Act of 1930. A children's court was opened at Rangoon under a stipendiary magistrate with special training and interest in social

The Dhammathats envisaged close-knit families in which the children lived under the gentle control and the loving care of the fathers – the nominal heads – and the mothers, the real managers of family affairs. The boys could leave on marriage, which they could contract on attainment of puberty, and the girls could also go when they reached their majority, or married with parental consent. Among filial duties owed to the parents by the children are the living together in the home, rendering service, obedience and respect, and sharing in the work and responsibilities of the family. In the village, the boy or the girl goes to the field with the parents while quite young, looks after the cattle, draws water from the well, gathers in the firewood, pounds the rice for food. These duties which custom recognizes have, to some extents, become obsolete in modern conditions of life where the boys and girls may have to leave the home for higher studies in the cities, or seek employment there, maintaining only the weakest links with the parents by weekly or monthly letters, and visits during the long vacations. Education in the monastery has also fallen out of fashion in the urban areas, and the novicehood in the Buddhist order which a boy goes through by tradition is also fast becoming a thing of the past.

Among the children equality is the rule, though the Dhammathats spoke of various modes of partition among them, sometimes favouring the oldest son, sometimes the oldest daughter, and, occasionally, the youngest child, male or female. Elaborate and varying rules seemed to have been set at various times. "Where there are daughters only, the eldest first takes the mother's clothes, and ornaments; the bulk of the estate, together with the father's clothes and ornaments, should be divided into 20 portions and the eldest daughter takes one. The remainder should again be divided into 20 portions and the second daughter takes one; and so on, three times, or, according to some, seven, or, as many times as there are daughters. The ultimate residue is equally divided among them all. When there are sons only, the eldest first takes the father's clothes and ornaments; the successive apportionment is here into ten shares. Where there are both sons and daughters, the eldest son takes the father's clothes and ornaments, the eldest daughter takes the mother's, and the divisions are into 15 shares."[1] These confusing rules have been rendered obsolete. Even at the time of the Manugye they had become unacceptable, for the best and sim-

work, and after a few years of experimental operation in a limited jurisdiction, the operation of the Act has been extended to the major urban areas, with new children's courts in Mandalay and other cities.

[1] *Kinwunmingyi Digest*, I, pp. 207–215.

plest test was fairness and equality in the interests of the family, as Manu, the wise one, said: "I will give an instance, it is just as when a hen brings food, all the chickens get an equal share to eat."[1] At least that would be the expectation among the chickens, though the largest share might go to the fastest one.

The Orasa, or Aurasa as the spelling also goes, is a departure from the rule of equality among the children. This Pali word means a child that comes from the breast, a natural child of love, and the Dhammathats gave more meaning to the word, and Orasa means today the eldest-born child who is capable of undertaking the responsibilities of a deceased parent. The Orasa may be the eldest son, or the eldest daughter and he or she has a special position because, in the quaint language of the Dhammathats, the parents "obtained the child by their earnest prayers at the commencement of their wedded life, and acquired the property with his or her assistance." The Privy Council, after examining the Dhammathats, held that there were three essential conditions for the existence of the status of Orasa: that the child is the first born; the child attains majority; the child, being a son, helps in the acquisition of the family properties and the discharge of the father's responsibilities, or, being a daughter, helps the mother in the management and control of family properties and household."[2] The status of Orasa is probably traceable to Hindu origins, but there is also the maxim of Burmese family life, which has it that the eldest son steps into the place of the father and the eldest daughter steps into the place of the mother, which may be its root.

On attainment of the status of Orasa, the eldest son, or the eldest daughter, acquires a vested right to one-fourth of the estate left to to the surviving parent by the parent whose place he or she takes – in the eyes of the law – on the death of that parent. The claim for the Orasa share may be made within 12 years of the death of the parent.[3] Modifying the Privy Council opinion, it has now been settled that the real test of the Orasa is not his or her helping to acquire the family property or manage family affairs, but competence to undertake the responsibilities of the deceased parent, should he or she be called upon to do so. "Joint living with the surviving parent and active assistance in his or her duties is not necessary under modern conditions," and, for example, if a son is "ready and willing to help in

[1] May Oung, *Leading Cases*, p. 231.
[2] *Kirkwood vs. Maung Thein*, 2 Ran. 693 P. C.
[3] *U Tauk Ta vs. Ma Ohn Yin*, 1939 RLR 217.

the acquisition of family property though not required to do so, or if he complies with requests to do so within the limits of his ability and in good faith, he has shown the degree of required competence."[1]

It has been suggested that the institution of Orasa in the Burmese family is an anachronism, belonging rightly to "ancient times when people lived the whole of their lives in one district, and for the most part in one village, when all the members of the family lived together (if not in unison) and 'ate out of the same dish' and when the father had patriarchal authority over the whole family." Today, however, "vast changes have taken place in the environment, circumstances, and habits of the Burmans since those far-off days when the Dhammathats were compiled. Families no longer live, as a matter of course, under the same roof; the days of the patriarch are numbered; and it has been judicially determined that under modern conditions it is not essential that the Orasa should live with the rest of the family or take part in the acquisition of the family property."[2] The "vested right" of the Orasa, the conditions to establish that status, and such related questions, remain to be fully tested in the light of changed conditions of society. In these days of equality when people are equally poor, big land holdings having been nationalized and big business – which never existed in Burma – having been effectively nipped in the bud by laws, the Orasa has little to gain by claiming his special share, and test cases of his present status and rights have not come to the courts.[3]

The Dhammathats mention twelve classes of children, those belonging to six being entitled to inherit the property of the parents, and those who fall in the remaining six being disqualified. Modern times and the changed circumstances of society and the family have rendered the classifications largely obsolete. Only some of the principal classes remain valid, as we shall see in a later chapter, and those classes which have passed out of currency retain their value only as exhibits in the museum of social history. The Manugye describes the following classes of children who have the right to inherit: "1. children born of a union contracted by parental authority, and known as *Orasa;* 2. children adopted publicly with a view to inherit, and known as *Keittima;* 3. children by a concubine who does not 'eat out of the same dish' with

[1] *Daw E vs. Maung Aung Thein,* 1941 RLR 665 F. B.

[2] *Maung Thein Maung vs. Ma Kywe,* 13 Ran. 412 F. B.

[3] E. g. The Land Nationalization Act, 1953, under which agricultural land has been taken over by the state and distributed to peasants, with 50 acres as the largest holding for one family, though the Burmese system of the joint family is also recognized, and in the case of a joint family it may hold as many 50-acre lots as there are families in it.

the husband, and known as *Hetthima* (the woman who is taken to wife during the lifetime of the chief wife, and who does not 'eat out of the same dish' with the husband is called an Apyaung, *i. e.* a concubine; (children of such a concubine are here meant); 4. children by a female slave of the husband or of the wife, or by a female slave bought out of joint property, such children are known as *Khettaja;* 5. children of the husband or the wife by a former marriage, and known as *Pubbaka;* and 6. children casually adopted, whether their parents and relatives are known or not, such children are termed *Apatitha.*"

The six classes of children who are not entitled to inherit are: "1. child who was given away by the parents and was brought up by others, and known as *Paradinna;* 2. child who was bought, and known as *Sahoddha;* 3. the wife separates from her first husband and marries another; after conception she returns to her first husband and gives birth to a child; the child so born, and known as *Punnanuggati;* 4. child begotten while in pursuit of amorous pleasure, and known as *Kilita;* child who is disobedient and behaves like an enemy, and known as *Swanutta;* and 6. destitute and hunger-stricken child fed and brought up in the family, and known as *Chatabhatta*".[1]

A concubine, as it will be apparent from the above, has a recognized status, though only as an "inferior" or "lesser" woman than the wife or wives. The permissibility of polygamy makes the terms somewhat confusing, and the western notions and prejudices brought in by the British judges did not help to make the situation easier. Earlier prejudice against polygamy led the judges to readily consign women other than the chief wife to concubinage. "I should be inclined to say," remarked Sir Harvey Adamson, chief justice of the Chief Court of Lower Burma, in an opinion that was later quoted with approval by the Privy Council, "that if a woman co-habits with a Burman whom she knows to be the lawful husband of another woman, the presumption is that she is a mistress and not a wife..."[2] The true position was established however, in a later decision which found that "a Burman Buddhist may have at the same time two or more wives, who are on an equal footing, though one of them may be styled the head wife, and her status may be superior to that of a free concubine, and that when a *maya nge* is mentioned in the Dhammathats, it is such a wife that is referred to and not a free concubine... Polygamy proper is undoubtedly coming to be looked on with more and more disfavour, but it is by no means

[1] *Kinwunmingyi Digest,* I, pp. 29–32.
[2] *Ma Wun Di vs. Ma Kin,* 4 LBR 175 P. C.

extinct even in Lower Burma, where it is not very uncommon for the daughter of respectable parents to be openly given in marriage with great ceremony to a man who already has one wife. In Upper Burma, before the annexation, polygamy was more common, especially amongst the official class. Only one wife was recognised by the King and received at the palace. She was called the *pwe-det* or *pwe-win* (approved wife). But the other wives were treated with respect by others than the royal family."[1]

When there are more wives than one, every wife – *maya* – wishes to describe herself as the *maya gyi*, the chief or head, and call the others *maya nge*, the "little or small," and in Burma, as elsewhere, women do not regard the entry of other women into their men's lives, in ways big or small, with any enthusiasm. The name-calling thus gets confused sometimes with the names. A second wife, even if taken after the death of the first, may sometimes be called the *maya nge*, just to identify her as the one who comes after, in point of time, but that again is obviously an inexact and misleading usage. *Apyaung* is a concubine, whose children may inherit, and the Dhammathats, in their quaint and elaborate fashion, mention different grades and classes of concubine, e. g. the "free concubine" such as *tawpyaung*, but the classifications bore traces of the Hindu caste system, and were never fully valid in the Burmese family, except perhaps in the royal family circles. The children of a concubine may share in the inheritance, but not those born out of casual amorous pleasure, nor the Punnanuggati conceived by another man. The Dhammathats prescribe their tests of paternity, proving thereby that the learned writers were wise not only in the academic law but in the more practical affairs of life as well. "Pregnancy cannot be caused by may men," points out Manugye, "the child is his at the time of whose intercourse the three causes combined," and the three causes are " the proper season of the woman; copulation with a man; the release of a fate by the death of some animal: the fate is not a life, not vivifying principle not a soul, but the ground of good or bad deeds that is to influence the new being through life, the balance of good or bad, for or against, the animal dying."[2]

The fate may be released from any being in the animal kingdom, a human being for example, and in its fast orbit round the earth it searches for a new home which will be where the woman is season combines with the man and where the fate is fated to come to rest. This is

[1] UBR (1910–13), 111.
[2] Richardson's translation of the Manugye, p. 296.

what a former Chief Justice of Burma had to say from his own personal family life. "We Buddhists believe that when a person dies, he goes either to the *nat-pye* (the abode of the celestial beings) or the *nga-ye-pye* (the nether world), or else is reborn as a human being or in the animal kingdom. There is a strong belief... that a dying person sometimes experiences premonitory visions of his destination. For instance, if on his death a person is to go to the heavenly world, he will see heavenly cars coming to convey him thereto. If, on the other hand, he is to go to the nether world, he will see inhuman beings coming to drag him away with them. In order to enable a person to go to the nat-pye we generally say prayers, chant *pirith*, and recite stanzas from the *Mingla Sutta* (Buddhist scriptures) by his side. By so doing, we help the dying person, if conscious, to concentrate his thought and mind on Lord Buddha, His Dhamma and His Sangha. During the last moments of my wife's life, both my mother-in-law and I, overwhelmed with grief, forgot to say prayers. We just remained silent by her side. Suddenly, my wife started shouting, 'Mother, Mother, there are big black men coming into the room to take me away with them. Please save me, please save me!' I realized then that the black men were the denizens of the nether world and that they had come to take away the soul of my wife; we could not see them because of their supernatural powers. I said to my mother-in-law, 'Please say prayers and recite mantras.' She did, and I also recited prayers... and my wife said, 'The black men have run away. Oh, now I see *nat-tha-mee* (fairy spirits) coming into the room to take me away... I now shikoe you, Mother, and I shikoe you, Ko Ba U. Please forgive any sins I may have committed.' So saying she passed away."[1]

Family planning is becoming better known in Burma, and among the middle class families it has become a proper subject for discussion. Since it is a little difficult to discover – and avoid – the millions of fates that are released all the time to fly round in search of homes, "modern" families resort to western science in their family planning.

2. ADOPTED CHILDREN

Adoption is an honoured institution among Burmese families. The motives are the ancient and universal ones: love, the need of man for solace and company, or for an extra hand in agricultural work, for a

[1] Dr. Ba U, *My Burma*, pp. 80–81.

man to lend masculine strength and leadership in the home, for a woman to add her feminine softness and her managerial skill.

Though the Dhammathats mention, as we have seen above, several classes of adoptive children, there are only two which have practical importance today: the Keittima and the Apatitha.

Any person who is competent to contract can adopt a child. A Buddhist monk, being bound by the Vinaya not to have natural children, cannot adopt a child.[1] In the case of a married couple, adoption must be by mutual consent of the husband and the wife, for the adoptive child comes in for inheritance and the Burmese customary law does not permit the distribution of property by will.[2] Adults may be adopted, though their adoption would be unusual, and funny movies have been made about an elderly bachelor who adopted an adult girl with the foreseeable consequences.

The status of a Keittima child in the family is close to that of a natural child. The intention of the adoptive parents must be clear that the child is brought into the family as a Keittima, and to establish this there should be publicity and notoriety – even as husband and wife establish their status by open conduct such as eating together in public – following the taking in of the child. These are matters of fact which must be proved when there is dispute whether a child is a Keittima, or merely a casually adopted Apatitha, whose rights of inheritance are inferior, or only a foundling who is taken into the home and reared out of pity and compassion, whose rights of inheritance may not even exist.[3] "Mere proof of adoption is not proof of Keittima adoption and mere description of someone by a person as his or her adopted child is not by itself an expression of intention that the child shall inherit. There must be some circumstances to show that the adoption was not an Apatitha adoption merely, but an adoption with a view to inheritance."[4] And Burmese social custom renders it necessary "to proceed with caution, for it is common knowledge that the Burmese are given to hospitality and are extremely liberal to relations, near or distant nephews and nieces and cousins of all degrees are taken into the family and generally provided for; and it is often a matter of some difficulty to distinguish between them and the sons and daughters of the house. In examining the evidence, therefore, two questions should be kept in

[1] *Ma Kyin Sein vs. Maung Kyin Htaik*, 1940 RLR 783.
[2] *Aung Ma Khaing vs. Mi Ah Bon*, 9 LBR 163.
[3] *Ma Me Gale vs. Ma San Yi*, LBR 172 P. C.; *Ma Ywet vs. Ma Me*, 5 LBR 118 P. C.; *Maung Ba Pe vs. Maung Shwe Ba*, 6 Ran. 520 P. C.
[4] *Ma Than Nyunt vs. Daw Shwe Thit*, 14 Ran. 557.

view: whether the treatment testified is not consistent with the view that the alleged adoptee was a favoured relative or dependant or, if not, whether it can be gathered from the adopter's conduct that he or she intended to confer heirship.[1]

The Registration of Adoptions Act of 1926 sought to clear up doubts and reduce disputes in inheritance by providing that no dispute as to the right of any person to inherit as or through a Keittima son or daughter should be entertained by any Court unless the fact of adoption was evidenced by an instrument of adoption executed by the adoptive parents and the adopted person (if that person was below the age of 20, by persons whose consent was required to effect the adoption under Burmese customary law), duly attested by two witnesses, and registered with the Registrar of Deeds. The Act, though passed, was not brought into operation. The Registration of Keittima Adoptions Act, operative from the 1st. April, 1941, has replaced the Act of 1926. The substance of the new Act remains much the same, except that the age at which an adopted person can execute the deed of adoption without the consent of his natural parents or guardians has been lowered from 20 to 18.

A Keittima child owes the same filial duties to his adoptive parents as a natural child does, and it has been held that failure to discharge those duties may forfeit him of the right to inherit.[2] It has also been thought that a Keittima must live in the home of the adoptive parents, but these matters of living together and discharging filial duties must weigh lightly these days.[3] A Keittima cannot acquire the status of Orasa, for however close he may be to the status of a natural child, the fact remains that he does not come from the breast; but again, this is a matter of no apparent value in modern times.[4] In an inheritance suit, an adoptive child may claim as an Apatitha child if he cannot furnish enough evidence to establish his status as a Keittima, and neither the Registration Act, nor any other law, prohibits him from taking that course.[5]

[1] May Oung, *Leading Cases*, p. 131.
[2] *Maung Aing vs. Ma Khin*, 2 UBR (1893) p. 22.
[3] In *Ko Pe Kyai vs. Ma Thein Kha*, 1937 Ran. 426, it was held that a Keittima child did not need to live with the adoptive parents in order to inherit as the parents intended from the start that he should inherit, but that an Apatitha child who lived apart did not earn the right to inherit.
[4] *Maung Po An vs. Ma Dwe*, 4 Ran. 184 F. B.
[5] *Daw Khin Nyun vs. Lim Geok Soe*, 1956 BLR 248 H. C.; *Chan Eu Ghee vs. Mrs. Iris Maung Sein*, 1953 BLR 294 H. C.

CHAPTER SIX

PROPERTY OF THE FAMILY

1. COMMUNITY OF PROPERTY

Sharing is the important element in the Burmese family. The husband and the wife share in the toils of earning and of running the home; they share in the fruits of their labours, and where one has brought property in at marriage or after as a gift received, or by succession, for example, the other too acquires a share in the property. In the joint earnings there is even more sharing. This principle of community flows from the status of women and the social custom which acknowledges their role as partners to their men.

This position puzzled the British judges who were at pains at first to discover the exact nature and extent of the community of interests. Did the husband and the wife hold the property as joint-owners, or as tenants in common? How separate was the "separate" property of each spouse, how joint was the joint property? Was the partnership a genuine one in the sense of modern partnership law, brought into Burma as the Partnership Act, and if so could one partner be made responsible for the debts that the other contracted on his or her own; if not, why not?

Before the trend of judicial thinking on those questions is traced it may be desirable to take a brief look at the various classes of family property, some of which have by their very nature become obsolete. *Kanwin* property is defined as the "marriage portion" or gifts received by the bride and the bridegroom from parents, and, these days, relatives and friends as well. While the Dhammathats speak of the Kanwin property as marriage portion, they speak also of dowry in the same breath, and perhaps, in the same sense as well. *Payin* is the property brought into the marital home by either the wife or the husband, and it retains some separate identity. The term was held to be applicable more to the separate property brought by a spinster and a bachelor, *Nge-lin-nge-maya*, into the home, than to the property brought by *Eindaunggyi* couple, i.e. where either or both the spouses had been married before. *Atetpa* is property brought by such Eindaunggyi couple, and its separate identity is held to be stronger than that of Payin. *Lettetpwa* is property which accrues to the family through one or both of the spouses, by inheritance, by gift, or earned by work and skill. Where the property is jointly acquired it is called *Hnapazon* which is, thus, a kind of Lettetpwa.

The classes of family property may be different, but the governing rule is that of community of interest. A happy home is where the husband and the wife share alike the toils and the fruits. "It is only when both husband and wife are equally good and virtuous and clever and wise, and when one is the helpmate of the other, both trying to acquire (and garner) property jointly and agreeably, that they are well and harmoniously matched like the soil and the rain, or gold and emerald, and will assuredly obtain many children, have several slaves and attendants, and get more and more prosperous like the rising sun and the waxing moon."[1] The general rule is that the spouses hold equal interests in all Lettetpwa property, except property inherited or received as gift by either spouse. It has been argued that where "the husband alone earns the income, while the wife does nothing," e.g. the earnings of a lawyer, a goldsmith, artisans, salaried officials and professional men, the wife's interest should only be one-third and not half of the earnings, but the rule of community goes not by who brings in the earnings but whether "the husband and wife prove to be helpmates to each other, both in prosperity and adversity," and if they do, then "they shall divide the property equally between them if they mutually desire to separate."[2] Hnapazon is thus a term that is liberally construed, and in most cases Lettetpwa and Hnapazon are interchangeable terms with both spouses enjoying equal shares in the property.

The rule of community applies in full to Payin property brought into the family by a virgin couple. The rules prescribed by the Dhammathats, it has been held, "disclose a very strong community of interest in the case of a first marriage and indicate that all property is joint, though the respective interests may vary in amount." In the case of an Eindaunggyi family, however, the Atetpa property may be held separately. "In the case of a first marriage there are no interests to be considered other than those of the husband and wife and of their children. But where either or both has been married before, it is likely that there will be children of the first marriage and their interests have also to be considered. That is a very good reason for not giving to each spouse the same rights in the Payin property of the other as are given

[1] E Maung, *Burmese Buddhist Law*, p. 59; Kinwunmingyi Digest, II, p. 148.
[2] May Oung, *Leading Cases*, pp. 54–61; Kinwunmingyi Digest, II, p. 166.

on a first marriage."[1] Payin is therefore regarded as a part of the joint property of the virgin couple, and the husband and the wife have each a one-third interest in the Payin brought into the home by the other spouse. Atetpa property brought by an Eindaunggyi couple may be held separate and disposed of separately. No rules of thumb can be valid, however, in this as in other family matters. The conduct of the parties and the facts in each case determine the measure of interests. Payin or Atetpa property may be converted, changed in character, and put into the family property as Lettetpwa. Or the property may be changed, but its character as Payin or Atetpa retained, such as when the husband sold a piece of land which he brought as Payin, and bought another piece of land which was held to be Payin still, and not Lettetpwa property.[2]

Thinthi is another class of property which a husband or a wife is supposed to hold separately, e.g. clothes, jewels or ornaments. It has also been held to cover *Minbe* property, or gifts made to either spouse by the King, a class of property which has obviously passed out of real life. The mention of Thinthi in the discussion of the interests of the husband and the wife in some of the texts seems to have been in error. "The various kinds of thinthi spoken of by the Dhammathats bear semblance to the exceptions grafted on the earlier Roman rule of proprietary incapacity of *filius familias*. The Dhammathats broadly define Thinthi as property which the children could hold as against their parents and which on the death of the parents could not be treated for purposes of inheritance and division as part of the estate of the parents."[3] It is difficult to point out an example of Thinthi property in the modern Burmese family.

The community of property in the Burmese family led the British judges to draw an analogy between it and partnership as they understood it. "The Buddhist law favours the equality of the sexes," Jardine observed, "and in many ways treats marriage as creating a partnership in goods."[4] From this it was but another step to hold that "a Burmese Buddhist husband and wife are partners and all the property of the

[1] *C. T. P. V. Chetty Firm vs. Maung Tha Hlaing*, 3 Ran. 322 F. B.; *U San Yi vs. Maung Po Yi*, 1940 RLR 534.; U Htan Hmat vs. U Ba Thein, Civ. Ap. 5/1961, decided by the Chief Court on April 19, 1962.

[2] *Maung San Dun vs. Ma Lok*, 6 BLJ 219; *U San Mya vs. U Tin*, 1935 AIR Ran. 129; but where Payin property was a piece of land occupied as a squatter, a subsequent grant of a lease during the coverture coverts the property into Lettetpwa, *Ma Pu vs. Maung Ngo*, 6 Ran. 234.

[3] E Maung, *Burmese Buddhist Law*, p. 63.

[4] *Ma Hla Aung vs. Ma E* (1883), S. J. 219.

marriage, whether Payin or Lettetpwa, is partnership property. The partnership is dissolved only by death or divorce and neither partner is entitled to separate possession of any share of the partnership property or of the profits until the partnership is dissolved... Either husband or wife or both may represent the partnership in dealing with the third person and a presumption ordinarily arises that debts contracted by either party bind the partnership and are recoverable out of the partnership property."[1] This view also led naturally to the thought that the joint properties were not partible – until death or divorce dissolved the partnership – and since they were indeterminate they were not saleable property in the eyes of the law.[2] These decisions led to confusion and hardship in business relations until a Special Bench of the High Court overruled them, and settled that "Burman Buddhists were in the habit of contracting marriages centuries before the law of partnership was in existence or contemplation, and there is no text relating to the customary law that could be cited to give colour to the notion that a Burmese Buddhist marriage is analogous to, if not identical with, an ordinary business partnership." They hold property "as tenants in common, not joint tenants. Each of them has a vested interest in such joint property, and such an interest is liable to attachment and sale in execution of a decree against the party entitled to it... Either party is competent to alienate or otherwise dispose of his or her own interest in the joint property, but neither of them is entitled to alienate the interest of the other without the consent, express or implied of that party." There is no presumption "*de facto* or *de jure*, that a Burmese Buddhist couple, living together, are agents for each other, or that the wife is deemed to consent to the acts of her husband. It is a fact to be determined according to the circumstances of each case."[3] The Privy Council has followed the ruling that husband and wife are tenants in common, on the ground that "as the Dhammathats do not point to joint ownership, rather than tenancy in common, it is right to prefer that alternative which leads to the least evil consequence."[4] Alienation of the wife's interest requires her consent. A husband cannot mortgage or sell the joint property – acquired by either of them before or during the marriage – except in circumstances in which it may properly be said that he has acted with the consent of his wife or as her agent.[5]

[1] *Ma Paing vs. Maung Shwe Hpaw*, 5 Ran. 296 F. B.
[2] *Ma Paing vs. Maung Shwe Hpaw*, 5 Ran. 478.
[3] *N. A. V. R. Chetty Firm vs. Maung Than Daing*, 9 Ran. 524 F. B.
[4] *U Pe vs. U Maung Maung Kha*, 10 Ran. 261, P. C.
[5] *Ma Ohn Kyi vs. Daw Hnin Nwe*, 1953 BLR 322 H. C.

But if the wife consents to her husband mortgaging the joint property as if it were his sole property, she is considered to hold him out to the mortgagee as her agent, not only in respect of the execution of the mortgage but also in respect of all subsequent transactions in connection with the mortgage.[1] Where a husband took out life insurance policies in his name and there was no evidence to establish whether the wife made any contribution to the payment of premia, it was held, on his being declared an insolvent, that "the rule of equal interest of husband and wife in all property acquired during coverture applied and the wife's half share in the policies did not vest in the Official Assignee."[2] The wife's right was one to obtain the proceeds of the policies, on their maturity or surrender, and it was a contingent right. In a case where a husband took out policies during coverture with one wife and he married again on her death, was held that the policies were not Lettetpwa property of the first marriage. Children of the first marriage, and the widow of the second were granted joint letters of administration by the lower Court, which, the High Court pointed out on appeal was "most inconvenient for the parties who are at loggerheads with each other," and it was ordered that letters be issued only to the widow.[3]

Sharing of the family property, and preserving property within the family where possible, are related motives and customs, and in the Burmese family there is the custom of pre-emption. A co-heir has the right of option to buy the share in undivided inherited property of another co-heir who wishes to sell. The right is that of being preferred to a stranger, the right of first refusal.

It was debated at one time whether pre-emption was not a matter to be decided by the ordinary civil law, instead of Burmese customary law, as one relating to options and sales. The Full Bench of the Chief Court of Lower Burma decided, on a reference, that it was an incident of inheritance, a right that co-heirs could invoke and "not confined to the case of undivided ancestral property, the desire to keep the property in the family being widespread and acted on by Burman Buddhists." It was decided that the right extended to "inherited immoveable property", not "ancestral" property alone, but a sale made to a stranger without an offer being first made to co-heirs was voidable, not void. Co-heirs must protest within a reasonable time, and pay the price for which the property has changed hands. Otherwise, the right is lost.

[1] *U Rai Gyaw Thoo & Co. vs. Ma Hla U Pru*, 1940 RLR 180, *Daw Nyein Mya vs. U Ba Ohn*, 1958 BLR 248 H. C.

[2] *The Official Assignee vs. Ma Hnin San*, 1940 RLR 208 F. B.

[3] *Daw Chit Ngwe vs. Maung Thein Aung*, 1955 BLR 157 H. C.

In the case it was held that the right extended not to land alone, but the trees on the land also, as "trees are permanently attached."[1] The decision left the question open as to who should be included in the term co-heirs; the case was one brought by persons who had jointly inherited ancestral property, and the Court had no difficulty holding they were co-heirs who enjoyed the right of pre-emption. When a husband dies, and the widow sells a piece of land, a son, not being the Orasa, cannot claim the right of pre-emption, since he is not a co-heir with the mother.[2] When, however, a mother remarries, and later the step-father marries again on her death, the children can claim their shares and the right of pre-emption.[3]

2. PARTITION ON DIVORCE

While it is now settled that during coverture the husband and the wife have their interests in the joint property, each having a right to alienate his or her share, it is on partition on divorce, or succession at the death of one spouse, that the interests stand out sharp and clear. A wife has a share in a plot of land which forms part of the joint property during the coverture, and she may sell the share or the interest; yet, it is open to dispute which part of the land is her's and which the husband's. It is usual in such dealings, therefore, to have both the husband and the wife execute the deeds of sale and join in having the deeds duly registered.

Partition on divorce usually goes by mutual consent, or settlement under arbitration of friends and elders. When the parties cannot come to terms, and go to the courts for decrees, partition is generally determined by the grounds for the divorce, the party at fault being liable to forfeit some shares to which he or she would otherwise have been entitled. The Dhammathats speak of partition and divorce as one transaction and the British judges at first thought that a suit must be founded on both as one inseparable cause of action. As we have noticed, the view has changed, and a suit for a "bare divorce" lies.

It is customary, even where there has been matrimonial fault which the Courts would recognize and found a decree on, for the parties to bring in the indispensable elders and talk things over, and after attempts

[1] *Ye Nan vs, Aung Myat San.* 8 LBR 466 F. B.

[2] *Maung Ba Cho vs. Maung San Tin,* 2 Ran. 437; *Maung San Tin vs. Ma Phet Pu,* 2 Ran. 659.

[3] *Maung Po Thaung vs. Maung E Pe,* 2 Ran. 529.

at reconciliation have failed, to draw up the divorce deed embodying the terms of the settlement. Such a deed, to be admissible in evidence, must bear stamps under the Stamp Act for the Government must also have its share in the partition.

The rule of dependency comes into play in partition on divorce by mutual consent. It applies to provide the party who has not brought much property, Payin or Atetpa, with a share from the property of the richer spouse. In such a situation, the richer spouse is the *Nissaya* or supporter, and the poorer is the *Nissita*, the supported or the dependant. "If the wife is dependent on the husband," says the Waru Dhammathat, "the husband shall obtain, when they separate by mutual consent, two-thirds of their property." The wife takes the remaining one-third. "If the husband and wife both belong to the official class," says Manugye, "and if they mutually desire to separate, each shall take his or her official badges and insignia and other personal clothes and ornaments. Of the rest of the animate and inanimate property, whoever supplies the greater part of the capital by the employment of which property is acquired, shall receive two-thirds of the property so acquired. The remaining one-third shall be taken by the person who supplies the rest of the capital."[1] The rule of Nissaya and Nissita was originally designed in the Dhammathats, it was thought, to apply to Payin property of a virgin couple, Nge-lin-nge-maya, but it seems to have been extended by judicial decision to the Eindaunggyi couple also, and it has been held that where one spouse has been previously married, and the other not, the Atetpa property of the party previously married should be divided on the principle of dependency provided no property has been acquired by the couple after the marriage. The principle, it was added by E Maung, J., should not be extended to a divorce which is not in fact by mutual consent but which for the purposes of partition is deemed, by legal fiction, to be one.[2]

On divorce by mutual consent, the parties to a Nge-lin-nge-maya marriage take back their Payin properties, while if they are Eindaunggyi they take back their Atetpa properties.[3] If the relationship of Nissaya and Nissita exists, then the dependant takes a third of the Payin or Atetpa of the other spouse. Where there are joint properties of the marriage, the parties share in them equally.[4] In the case of Lettetpwa

[1] *Kinwunmingyi Digest*, II, pp. 166–167; O. H. Mootham, *Burmese Buddhist Law*, Oxford University Press, 1939, p. 43.

[2] *Maung Sein Bwint vs. Ma Than Sein*, 1948 BLR 1.

[3] *U San Yi vs. Maung Po Yi*, AIR 1940 Ran. 286.

[4] *Maung Hmon vs. Maung Meik*, 2 UBR 1.

property acquired by succession by one spouse, the other is entitled to receive a third share.

Partition goes as if the divorce is by mutual consent when it is based on the cruelty of one spouse, and this is one example of how legal fiction works. Where, however, cruelty takes an aggravated form and the guilty party, instead of being repentant, seeks the divorce, or drives the other to seek it by repeated acts of cruelty, then the guilty party is liable to forfeit his or her share of the joint property on divorce.[1]

There has been a vague notion that where a divorce is adjudged through the fault of one party, the innocent party obtains all the property, including the joint property and the separate property of the guilty spouse. This notion was accepted in a case where a deserted wife sued for divorce and partition claiming one-third of certain properties inherited by the appellant during the marriage and one-sixth of estimated profits thereon during the three years of desertion. Both the District Court and the High Court granted the partition, holding that in strict law the wife could have claimed the whole of his property, except the interest therein of the first wife of the guilty spouse. The Privy Council considered that the proposition "which the Courts in Burma adopted as the basis of their judgement, viz. that because the defendant deserted the plaintiff, she was entitled to divorce with possession of all the husband's interest in the property... is in itself a startling proposition, and if adopted would have very far-reaching effects. There is no text in the Dhammathats or in the Burmese Buddhist Law books to support it, there is no case law on the subject..." It was ruled that the facts of each case needed to be examined such as, in the case, the fact that the husband married the wife by misrepresenting that he had no previous marriage, that the desertion was of an aggravated nature and quite unjustifiable and "that desertion, where there is a duty to comfort and support, is regarded by the Burmese as a serious offence." The Privy Council decided that in that case, the partition granted was in accord with justice and equity, deserving to stand.[2]

Just as a husband guilty of desertion does not necessarily lose his shares of the family property, a wife too does not forfeit her interests by the mere act of desertion. The facts of the case and the gravity of the offence will be relevant factors to consider in the partition, and generally, the divorce will be regarded, by a legal fiction, as one by mutual consent.

[1] *Daw Pu Gyi vs. Maung Tun Kha,* 1946 Ran. 125.
[2] *Maung Po Nyun vs. Ma Saw Tin,* 5 Ran. 841 P. C.

Adultery by the wife is a ground for divorce, and being a personal cause of action, it is for the husband only, and not strangers, to invoke.[1] It has been held that a wife forfeits her share in the Hnapazon and Lettetpwa property when partition is effected on divorce, though with regard to other property the divorce may be regarded as one by mutual consent. Adultery must be admitted by the guilty wife, or proved, for the husband cannot retain the joint property on his own allegation of his wife's fault.[2]

Divorce raises problems of partition not of the properties alone but of the children as well.' It is for the parting parents to arrange and agree on which children should go with whom, the girls generally going with the mother, the boys with the father. Such parental agreements bind the minor children, and as the family is broken, and two separate families come into being, it has been thought that those who go with the mother lose their rights of inheritance to the father's estate, and those who go with the father lose their rights in the mother's estate. "There would be no reason why all natural affection should be extinguished between parent and child because there had been a separation of the parents, but that is a different matter from the maintenance of the family bond constituting the title to inherit... Now it appears to be clearly a principle of Buddhist law that the child who is to inherit must aid and cherish the parent, and live with him or under such circumstances as to show that filial duty is discharged according to his wishes and that the family tie is kept unbroken."[3] Visiting is not sufficient to establish a resumption of the family tie. There must be clear proof of the taking in of the child, the full and clear flow of filial relations.

In these days when living together is not a rigid requirement, and the discharge of filial duty somewhat lightly construed, the rights of a child to inherit from his divorced parents will be liberally, rather than restrictively, viewed. In a case where the parents had parted by mutual consent, when their son was 34 years old, and the mother came to live with him while he maintained "filial relations" with his father also, the Supreme Court held that the son was not excluded from inheriting in the estate of the second wife of the father. "The law relating to the children of divorced parents has been greatly misunderstood," the Supreme Court observed." The law is mainly case law. Partly as a

[1] *Ma Dun Mai vs. Maung San Tun*, AIR 1938 Ran. 168.
[2] *U Sin vs. Ma Ma Lay*, 1941 RLR 14.
[3] *Ma Sein Nyo vs. Ma Kywe*, (1893) 2 UBR 159; *Ma Chit May vs. Ma Saw Shin*, 13 Ran. 166.

consequence of the Manugye having been incorrectly rendered in Richardson's translation... and partly as a result of deductions from the law relating to adoption of minor children, it has come to be enunciated that where parents effected a divorce with partition of property and arrangements by mutual consent were made for the custody or disposal of children after the divorce, the children who went with the father did not retain any right to a share in the mother's estate and *vice versa*." The rule of exclusion was not to be strictly applied. Even in the case of adopted children, it was pointed out, "by the time the Manugye came to be completed it was settled law that only minor children could be given in adoption without their wishes being consulted... And the right of the child so given away in its infancy to return to its natural family was recognized..."[1]

Guardianship of the person, or the property, of minor children is governed by the Guardian and Wards Act, and not by the Burmese customary law.[2] Where a guardian needs to be appointed to take care of a minor child, or represent his interests, the Court may consider the child's preference for guardian, but the paramount consideration is the minor's own welfare and happiness. Thus, in a case where a step-parent had entered a Buddhist family, and the need for appointing a guardian for a minor child arose, the Court recognized that the entry of a step-parent could be a disintegrating element under the circumstances, and after considering the qualifications of different persons for the guardianship, appointed the eldest sister of the minor child, in preference to the mother who had remarried.[3] The welfare and happiness of the minor, it has been ruled in the application of the Act, must weigh even against the rights of guardianship under the law to which the minor is subject. The father of an illegitimate child does not have a legal claim to his custody.[4]

3. MAINTENANCE

One of the five duties which the Dhammathats define for the husband to discharge towards the wife is "to provide her with proper clothes and ornaments." With worldly wisdom, and carefully borrowing the

[1] *U Aung Kywe vs. Maung Po Hla Win*, 1952 BLR 15 S. C.
[2] *C. T. V. E. V. Chettyar vs. Ma Saw Mwe*, 12 Ran. 47; *Dawsons Bank Ltd. vs. Ma May*, 12 Ran. 656.
[3] *Tee Swee Kyu vs. Chan Chain Lyan*, 1947, RLR 107.
[4] *U Maung Maung vs. Ma Aye Bu*, 1952 BLR 406 H. C.

authority of the Buddha, the Dhammathats also point out that "feminine nature being such that if a woman is not permitted to manage the house and prepare the meals she gets annoyed although she may be provided with the best dresses and ornaments; so, the Buddha who knew this, taught that women should be allowed the management of the house."[1]

To provide for the wife is not a moral duty only but a legal duty also. If, while the husband and the wife are living apart during the marriage he fails to support her in the accustomed standards of life, she has the right to sue in the civil courts for maintenance. The Privy Council held in an early case that the duty of the husband to "provide subsistence, and to furnish her with suitable clothes and ornaments" gave rise to a cause of action on its breach.[2] In a later case, the High Court in Rangoon heard and rejected a clever argument that since a Burmese Buddhist husband and wife held properties jointly, a suit by the wife for maintenance was an impermissible indirect means employed by her to obtain some part of her share in the joint property while reserving her right to a full share in the remainder. It was pointed out that "marriage, whatever the form of the contract may be, constitutes, if not an express, at all events an implied contract between the parties that the husband shall maintain his wife." In Christian marriages in the earlier times when the husband and the wife were one in the eyes of the law, the husband being the one, the wife could not sue for maintenance, but the High Court pointed out that this principle never applied in Burmese customary law. There being a legal duty for the husband to maintain the wife, failure to perform the duty gives rise to a cause of action for a civil suit, and maintenance may be asked for under the Civil Procedure Code from the day the suit is instituted, but not before.[3]

The "positive legal duty" of the Buddhist husband to maintain his wife being established, the High Court has gone further to point out that "the nature of the implied term from which that duty arises makes it in one respect more onerous than the corresponding duty of an English husband... who when sued for maintenance has a good defence if he pleads and proves that before action brought the wife deserted him without just cause, that being a breach of the contract of marriage going to its root. But (in Burmese customary law) no marital offence

[1] *Kinwunmingyi Digest,* II, 104.
[2] *Maung Hmun Taw vs. Ma Pwa,* (1884) S. J. 258 P. C.
[3] *Ma Saw Nwe vs. U Aung Soe,* 1939 RLR 527.

by the wife can take away during the subsistence of the marriage her proprietary rights which, though precarious as regards amount, vested indefeasibly at the moment she married. In other words, the Buddhist husband is sued not *qua* husband but *qua* manager, and no wrong done to him in the former capacity can benefit him in the latter." The High Court decided that Burmese customary law entitled the wife to sue for one-third of the husband's monthly income. "With regard to amount, a wife in England is as a general rule allowed by way of maintenance the amount necessary to bring her own income up to one-third of the parties' combined incomes. By a pure, but curious, coincidence one-third is the quantum of her interest in Burmese Buddhist law in property acquired by the exertions of a monogamous husband." While the wife may sue for maintenance, and the suit would be determined by Burmese customary law being clearly one related to marriage, a child, however, may not sue the father for maintenance. He did not get the right to sue, it was pointed out, from the Burma Laws Act which defined the scope of Burmese customary law, nor from "justice, equity and good conscience" – held to mean the English common law which did not permit a child to sue the parents for his maintenance. It was the mother's moral duty to maintain the child, and for the Court to take that factor into consideration in determining the amount of the maintenance.[1] A man may not take advantage of his own wrong, and raise the plea that he has deserted his wife to vacate a maintenance order that has been decreed against him.[2] The refusal of a wife to live with her husband does not forfeit her of the right to maintenance if she has reasonable grounds for her refusal, e.g. when the husband takes a second wife without her consent and expects the two wives to live under the same roof.[3] If a husband fails to provide the wife with suitable maintenance, he is liable for debts incurred by her for necessaries.[4]

Relief in the nature of maintenance may also been obtained by summary means under the Criminal Procedure Code. Section 488 provides that if any person "having sufficient means neglects or refuses to maintain his wife or his legitimate or illegitimate child unable to maintain itself, the District Magistrate, a Sub-divisional Magistrate or a Magistrate of the first class may, upon proof of such neglect or refusal, order such person to make a monthly allowance for the maintenance of his wife or such child, at such monthly rate, not exeeding one hundred

[1] *Dr. Tha Mya vs. Ma Khin Pu,* 1940 RLR 807.
[2] *Daw Khin Pu vs. Dr. Tha Mya,* 1949 BLR 283 H. C., F. B.
[3] *Ma Khin U vs. Po Saw,* 4 LBR 340 F. B.
[4] *Maung Hmum Taw vs. Ma Pwa.*

rupees in the whole, as such Magistrate thinks fit..." The wife loses the right to maintenance if she lives in adultery or refuses to live with her husband without sufficient reason, or if they are living separately by mutual consent. The summary procedure is designed to extend speedy relief to the wife to meet her minimum needs for food, clothing and shelter and to the children for their similar needs and simple essential education.[1] For maintenance to keep her in circumstances more becoming of her station in life, the wife must go to a civil court and file a suit.

A Buddhist monk – who has taken the vow of celibacy and poverty – does not escape the obligation to maintain a child born of illicit intercourse with a woman. The monk may have severed his ties with the mundane world, and, for some purposes, died "a civil death," but the Criminal Procedure Code overrides the customary law, and the obligations that it imposes remain un-extinguished by what the customary law or the Vinaya may say. The Courts have held that it would be against public policy to allow a monk to enter into such illicit relations without fear and with impunity so far as s. 488 of the Code is concerned.[2] Where, however, a husband puts on the yellow robes for four years, not merely to be a *Dunlaba Rahan* or priest for a brief period, but with the intention to "renounce the world" it is ruled that there is a severance of the marriage tie and no proceedings for maintenance may be taken, even on his return to the lay life.[3] If a wife applies for maintenance and the husband offers to live with her again, the Court must inquire into the reasonableness of her refusal – if she refuses to return to the husband – before it may dismiss her application.[4] To successfully defend himself against an application for maintenance on the ground that the wife has been "living in adultery" the husband must prove "a continuous course of guilty conduct and not isolated acts of immorality" on her part.[5]

As illegitimate children are also entitled to maintenance under s. 488 of the Code, questions of paternity often arise, and the Courts apply the usual standards of proof. It has been held, however, that the Code does not grant power to the Courts to have "blood tests" made of the child and the alleged father and an application for such tests made by the respondent who denies paternity will be rejected.[6]

[1] *Maung Shwe Ba vs. Ma Thein Nya,* 1938 RLR 673.
[2] *Maung Tun vs. Ma Hmin,* 11 Ran. 226 F. B.; *U Arzeina vs. Ma Khin Shwe,* 1940 Ran. 668.
[3] *Maung Nyunt Tin vs. Ma Pu,* 1954 BLR 76 H. C.
[4] *U Kin Yone vs. Ma Than,* 1954 BLR 365 H. C.
[5] *Maung Tin Hla vs. Ma Ngwe Sein,* 1954 BLR 242 H. C.
[6] *Fatima Bi Bi vs. A. M. Shrazi,* 1957 BLR 155 H. C.

4. INHERITANCE AND SUCCESSION

A Burmese Buddhist does not have the right to dispose of his property by means of a will. Inheritance, therefore, is by intestate succession only.

The British judges, after extensive survey and research, ruled early that though "there can be no doubt that Buddhists have for some years been disposing of their property by will, yet there is no evidence of such long established usage as would justify the conclusion that the power of testamentary alienation has become a recognized part of the Buddhist law."[1] The Local Government in British Burma studied the question extensively in 1881, and when a bill was proposed to declare the extent of the testamentary power of Hindus and Buddhists, and to provide for the exercise of that power, the Chief Commissioner reported that in Burma "there is a strong and general opinion against any considerable extention of the testamentary power. Mr. Egerton Allen, the Government Advocate, has endeavoured to trace the history of wills in British Burma. He stated that the earliest Buddhist will of which probate had been granted was made in 1864, that in 1865 the then Chief Commissioner, on being asked his opinion as to the expediency of extending to Buddhists such part of the Indian Succession Act as relates to testamentary succession, had stated that he considered that no part of that Act should be extended to Burma as the Buddhist law did not allow the making of any will, the terms of which might be at variance with the law of inheritance..."[2] The Committee on Buddhist Wills, appointed in 1938, also came to the same conclusions.

The Burmese customary law of inheritance governs the estate of Chinese Buddhists, Sino-Burma Buddhists – "if a Chinese Buddhist is prima facie governed by the Burmese Buddhist law there is all the more reason why a Sino-Burman Buddhist should be governed by the same"[3] – and every "Buddhist in Burma, irrespective of what his nationality is, and of whence he came."[4] Sino-Burmese Buddhists cannot make a will, but Chinese Buddhists have been considered to have the competence because the custom and usage governing them is different in this particular respect.[5] But the custom or usage must be proved,

[1] *Ma Bwin vs. Ma Yin*, 1878 SJLB 95; *Maung Me vs. Sit Kin Nga*, 1887 SJLB 429; S. Roy, *Customs, Customary Law in British India*, Calcutta, 1911, pp. 360-61.

[2] G. S. Henderson, *The Law of Wills in India*, Tagore Lectures, Calcutta, 1887, p. 6.

[3] *Chan Eu Ghee vs. Mrs. Iris Maung Sein*, 1953 BLR 294 H. C.

[4] *Daw Thike vs. Cyoung Ah Lin*, 1951 BIR 133 S. C.

[5] *Cyong Ah Lin vs. Daw Thike*, 1949 BLR 168 H. C.; *Yup Soon E vs. Saw Boon Kyaung*, 1941 RLR 285.

being foreign law, and to have the force of law it must be ancient, certain and reasonable, and, being in derogation of the general rules of law, must be construed strictly.[1]

The equality of women with men, and their role in the family as managers and sharers, is pointed out as the reason for the absence of testamentary power. "According to Burmese notions, the wife is considered as practically on an equality with the husband, and she generally takes an equal part in the mangement of the family affairs. Consequently, she has, for the most part, an interest equal to her husband's in the family property and when her husband dies this interest is carefully protected by the law of inheritance. In such a system, where the interest of a husband and wife in all property acquired during coverture is joint, and indivisible except on divorce, there seems to be no room for an institution which cannot but tend towards disturbing the harmony of wedded life."[2]

Though the will, as understood in English law, is unknown, "family compacts" or settlements may be made, either by word of mouth, or in writing, and these are respected and recognized by the courts even when the arrangements may not have been strictly according to the rules of succession, and even if there has been misconception of legal rights. Such arrangements may be made by the parents and the heirs, or the heirs after the death of the parents, and since the design of the compacts is to preserve peace and harmony in the family, they will be held valid in the absence of fraud or misrepresentation and such grounds for voiding contracts.[3]

"*Thedansa*" – record upon death – is a disposition of property, more or less in accordance with the ordinary rules of succession, made by the aged or dying owner. The "Thedansa" takes effect immediately, and as the Dhammathats say, "what the dead gave the living gets, and he whom the dead liberated is indeed emancipated."[4] When a Burman Buddhist husband makes an absolute gift of a property to a person, and the wife dies after the gift, and the husband inherits her share, then on the death of the husband, the son, as heir, cannot challenge the gift on the principle that a man cannot derogate from his grant.[5] But one cannot make a transfer *inter vivos* to take effect on his death, for that would amount to "disposing of his property after his death, con-

[1] *Daw Thike vs. Cyong Ah Lin*; Hla Aung, *Sino-Burmese Marriages.*
[2] May Oung, *Leading Cases*, p. 190.
[3] *U Myat Pyu vs. Ma Saw Shin,* 1949 BLR 492 H. C.
[4] *Kinwunmingyi Digest,* I, p. 133.
[5] *Maung Pan Myaing vs. Maung Tun Nyein,* 1949 BLR 338 H. C.

trary to the terms of the Buddhist law of inheritance."[1] Death-bed gifts may be challenged and nullified if they tantamount to distribution of property by will. Where a Sino-Burmese Buddhist made a gift of her entire estate nine days before her death to strangers, when there were natural heirs, the gift was declared invalid, for such a gift to a stranger, "even if accompanied by delivery of possession is invalid against natural heirs under Buddhist law as intended to defeat the personal law."[2] In order to prove a death-bed gift it must be shown first that the donor was in fact on his death-bed and second that he had no hope of recovery at the time of making the gift. In the absence of such circumstances there is no rule of law which prevents a sick man from disposing of every item of his property provided the gift is to take effect at once.[3] If immoveable property is transferred by way of gift, the deed of transfer must be registered under the Registration Act.[4] The Transfer of Property Act will also apply, e.g. ss. 122 to 129, to gifts.

Provident funds are governed by the prescribed Provident Fund Rules, and a subscriber may nominate members of his family to succeed to the funds. To that extent a subscriber has control of the direction by which the funds shall descend. He cannot, however leave his provident fund to anyone outside the family; if he has no family, he is entitled to leave the funds to a charitable institution.[5] He may not nominate heirs to the provident fund to the point of defeating the customary law provision against will-making.[6]

It has been aptly observed that the "Burmese customary law of inheritance as set forth in the Dhammathats is not strictly speaking a system of law but a congeries of decisions which are usually pronouncements *ad hoc* upon particular cases as they have arisen, and which, for the most part, do not purport to be determined persuant to any general or guiding principle. Much of this ancient law has become anachronistic, and the Courts from time to time have re-stated the common law of Burma in the light of new conditions of life that have come into being, discarding as obsolete ancient rules that no longer accord with the modern outlooks or the habits of the people. The present customs are a safer guide than the little known laws of the Dham-

[1] *Ma Thin Myaing vs. Maung Gyi*, 1 Ran. 351; *Maung Thu Kha vs. U Thunanda*, 5 Ran. 371.

[2] *Daw Thai vs. Daw Ngoot*, 1949 BLR 471 H. C.

[3] *U Kya Bu vs. Maung Aung Thein*, 1946 RLR 139.

[4] *Maung Pu vs. Tha Hpye*, 1948 BLR 717.

[5] *E. M. Hanney vs. E. F. Rodriguez*, 1941 RLR 712.

[6] *Ma Nu vs. Ma Gun*, 2 Ran. 388.

mathats."[1] The *ad hoc* decisions and rulings laid out in the Dhammathats fall outside the scope of this study. It will suffice to briefly outline the general principles of succession which have been extracted from the Dhammathats and prevailing customs by the courts over the decades.

One principle is that inheritance shall not ascend when it can descend. A descendant, however remote, will exclude an ascendant, however near. On the death of a brother or sister without leaving a spouse or issue, the younger brothers and sisters of the deceased inherit to the exclusion of the elders. The fact that a parent may be alive at the time of a child's death makes no exception to the rule.[2] In the words of the Dhammathats, thus, "a gift made by grandparents to their children or grandchildren shall not be resumed by way of inheritance on the death of the donees. Because a calf obtains its milk from the cow and not the cow from the calf."[3] The natural heirs of a Burmese Buddhist are, therefore, his or her widow or husband, and children; parents, brothers and sisters and their issue have, ordinarily, no right to share in the estate if the deceased leaves a single child or grand-child. Keittima adopted children, and to an extent the Apatitha child, step-children and even grandchildren, are preferred under this rule to ascendants.[4] Where, for want of descendants, inheritance must ascend, it should not do so more than is necessary.

"It is natural," says Razathat, "for sea-water to flow back into the ocean after entering rivers and streams," and in another passage, "when lakes are full, the overflow is returned to rivers and streams, and tidal water always flows back to the ocean." And Manu Vannana has this to illuminate the principle: "In the absence of wife and children, the parents inherit. Why so? Because, of the water which flows into the sea a portion returns up the river." These enunciations in "figurative language" the Privy Council found to "rather perplex than help the mind."[5] Out of these, however, and the customs of the people as they could be gathered, the first principle of non-ascent of inheritance, and the second, and related, principle of the nearer excluding the more remote were gleaned. "This principle applies to all cases of collateral succession... The Dhammathats lay down that only those who are

[1] Sir Arthur Page, C. J., in *Maung Thein Maung vs. Ma Kywe*, 13 Ran. 412 F. B.
[2] Mootham, *Burmese Buddhist Law*, p. 71; *Lim Kar Gim vs. Mrs. Iris Maung Sein*, 1955 BLR 15 S. C.
[3] *Kinwinmungyi Digest*, I, p. 377.
[4] May Oung, *Leading Cases*, p. 192.
[5] *Ma Hnin Bwin vs. U Shwe Gon*, 8 LBR 1 P. C.

'within reach of the inheritance' shall succeed, e.g. where A had two brothers, B and C, and B predeceased A, B's children would be excluded by C because their parent, at the time of his death, had no vested right; consequently they were 'out-of-time'. Similarly a grand-parent is postponed to a parent, an uncle or aunt to a brother or sister, and so on. But in the case of descendants, the rule is relaxed, and out-of-time grandchildren are permitted to share with their uncles and aunts; though the share is lessened, unless their parent had occupied the position of an Orasa with preferential rights."[1]

Other principles have been deduced from the two main ones: equidistant collaterals of the same level share equally; in a competition between equidistant collaterals of different levels the one on the lower level excludes the one on the higher; relatives of the full-blood are preferred to those of the half-blood. The full-blood is given one degree weightage over the half-blood; thus a brother of the full-blood excludes a brother of the half-blood; a brother and a sister of the half-blood stands within the same reach of inheritance as nephews and nieces of the full-blood.[2]

Succession cannot be kept in abeyance, and once it has vested cannot be divested.

It was thought at one time that joint living was necessary to entitle one to inheritance, but Burmese customary law, it has been established, does not give any meritorious value to mere living together and does not make the opposite state of things a reason for exclusion from inheritance. Where a claimant is a spouse of, or connected by blood with, the deceased mere separate living, without proof of actual division or of neglect in the performance of family duties, does not affect the rights to inherit. In the case of adopted children the duty to live together and perform their filial duties may rest a little heavier, though, as we have seen, in these days the requirements are loosely construed.

The general order of devolution of the estate of a deceased person will thus be: the surviving spouse, subject to the share of the Orasa, if any; the descendants; the first line of collaterals, namely brothers and sisters; the parents; the second line of collaterals, namely uncles and aunts, and in default, upon successive ascending lines of collaterals.[3]

Some illustrative cases and special situations may be looked at.

[1] May Oung, *Leading Cases*, p. 193.

[2] *Mrs. Kirkwood (a) Ma Thein vs. Maung Sein*, AIR 1938 Ran. 74; *Ma Galay vs. Ma E Mya*, 8 Ran. 23; *Maung Tun Zan vs. Maung Tun Zan Gyi*, AIR 1933 Ran. 317; *Daw Kyi Kyi vs. Ko Ko Lay*, 1958 BLR 195 H. C.

[3] Mootham, *Burmese Buddhist Law*, p. 75.

Where a married couple die within a short interval of each other – the short interval being judicially interpreted as a month or a little more in exceptional circumstances – then the relatives of both sides, irrespective of the degree of their relationship with the deceased husband or the deceased wife, are entitled to share in the half estate of each. This special rule arises from the notion that the joint estate of the couple still retains that character and "the succession would seem to be governed by accident, or by the caprice of fate, rather than a rule of law, if the relatives of the survivor exclude those of the spouse who died shortly before."[1] If a couple leaves behind parents, the parents of each shall receive the property taken by their respective child to the marriage; the jointly acquired property shall be divided equally; if one of the couple did not bring any property to the marriage, then the property brought by the other shall be divided into three shares and one share given to the parents of that party.

Where one of the couple dies, and the other survives, then, as we have seen, the surviving spouse inherits the estate, with the Orasa having a claim to a share. If the deceased had children by a previous marriage, the children may also share in the inheritance of their parental property.

When the surviving spouse dies, the children inherit, sharing equally – except for the preferential claims of the Orasa – and if there are no children, the grandchildren, and if there are no grandchildren, the great grandchildren inherit. When a daughter predeceases her parents, her husband who survives her does not inherit from the parents, though the out-of-time grandchildren may.[2]

When there are no natural descendants – children, grandchildren, or Keittima children and such – an Apatitha adopted child may inherit, and in the absence of such a child, step-children may come in.[3] In the absence of these descendants brothers and sisters come in, being preferred to parents. In the absence of parents, the grandparents inherit, and in the absence of these heirs, nephews and nieces, uncles and aunts, children of the nephews and nieces, cousins, etc. will inherit.[4] A stranger may inherit who looked after the deceased in health and sickness when he was deserted, or intentionally neglected, by the natural heirs, and such a stranger was held to even exclude the heirs.[5] While that may

[1] *Ma Ein vs. Tin Nga.* 8 LBR 197; *U Po Thu Daw vs. Maung Tin,* 8 Ran. 480.
[2] *Maung Kyi Oh vs. Maung Thet Pon,* 4 Ran 513 P. C.
[3] *Ma Sein Hla vs. Maung Sein Hman,* 2 LRB 54.
[4] *Ma Tin vs. Shwe Sint,* 4 Ran. 27 F. B.
[5] *Ma Mya vs. Maung Kywet,* 11 B. L. R. 228.

be of doubtful validity, it is accepted that the stranger may inherit at least in preference to the Government to whom the estate escheats in the total absence of heirs.

Complications may arise over inheritance when a man has more wives than one. "A man may marry as many as ten wives if he can maintain them all by his own skill and labour," permits the Dhammathats.[1] Fortunately or unfortunately, in these days of financial hardship, it would require a super-man to maintain ten wives by his skill and labour, and the problem of wives competing for inheritance is not of very great practical importance. For many years the Courts have remained tranquil and untroubled by the clamour of wives, each claiming to be the one and only love of the dear departed, that the others were frauds or maids of casual amorous acquaintance at the most, or if they were wives they were "inferior wives" and she alone the "chief" and the "superior". Facts must be carefully assembled and weighed to determine the status of each contender, and the concubines and casual acquaintances put out of the competition, before the interests of the "wives" can be correctly appraised. "Among Burman Buddhists when a man enters into and maintains conjugal relations with a woman whose position falls short of that of his first or chief wife, her connection with him must be shown to be such that she may be said to have been endowed with proprietary as well as personal rights before she can succeed to his estate. This is more so where she had prior knowledge of the first wife's existence and lived apart from her and unknown to her. Where T, a Burman Buddhist, has a wife in one place and keeps a woman Y at another place, who receives his visits unknown to the chief wife but with prior knowledge of the existence of the chief wife, Y taking no part on the business of T and not being publicly recognized as of an equal status with the chief wife, Y was at best an 'inferior' wife living separately from T and only receiving his visits and was thus not entitled to inherit any portion of T's estate."[2] On the other hand, there may be wives of equal standing who inherit equally and also "women of humbler standing who are differentiated from wives proper or 'superior' wives, who inherit as 'inferior' or 'lesser' wives. Such an inferior or lesser wife, if living together with the husband is entitled to two-fifths and the superior wife to three-fifths of the husband's estate; but where such inferior wife is living apart and is only occasionally visited by the husband, she is entitled to nothing more

[1] Kinwunmingyi Digest, II, p. 166.
[2] *Maung Tha Dun vs. Ma Thein Yin,* 1 Ran. 1.

than the property which had passed to her possession during the husband's life-time."[1] It is not what she is called, but what she is as established by the facts of the case that will, therefore, determine the status of a 'wife' and her share in the estate of the deceased 'husband'.

Where a Burman Buddhist Eindaunggyi, having two wives, inherits immoveable property from his father, after the second marriage, the property is the Lettetpwa of the marriages and is the joint property of the husband and wives, and not the separate property of the husband. The share of the two wives jointly is one-third, and since the two wives are of equal status, the share of each is one-sixth, which is a right that vests in each wife from the time the property is inherited by the husband.[2] This is a rule that may not remain exactly true today, having been overruled by the High Court, and reaffirmed, referred to and discussed, but it indicates the notions of social equity that find acceptance in the Burmese family.[3]

Burmese Buddhist heirs are tenants in common, not joint tenants, of the inheritance, and the only way in which one heir can obtain his share from another heir or heirs who are in possession of the property – in case there is a dispute – is by way of an administration suit, and not a suit for partition. In the administration suit, all the properties in the estate must be brought to an account. Consequently, if an heir is to get a share of the inheritance, a suit for a share of one property of the inheritance does not lie.[4]

When the claims of an applicant for letters of administration to the estate of a deceased person are admitted by other rival applicants, the Court normally grants the letters of administration to such applicant, provided he is a fit and proper person to administer the estate, and there is no necessity for the Court to consider the status of the rival claimants.[5] When, however, there is no such admission, the status of the claimants must be examined, before deciding who should have the administration of the estate. A husband would be entitled to administer the estate of the deceased wife, but if his status as such, or his fitness, is challenged, the Court must go into these issues.[6] Where a sister and an alleged adopted daughter apply, the Court may take up the question

[1] *Ma Thein Yin vs. Maung Tha Dun*, 2 Ran. 62.

[2] *C. T. P. V. Chetty Firm vs. Maung Tha Hlaing*, 3 Ran. 322 F. B.

[3] *N. A. V. R. Chettyar vs. Maung Than Daing*, 9 Ran. 524; *Daw Hla Ohn vs. Ma Nyun*, 1937 RLR 410.

[4] *Ma Pwa Shin vs. U PoSin*, AIR 1937 Ran. 24; *Daw Daw Shin vs. U Aung Pe*, 1957 BRL 5 H. C.

[5] *Ma Tok vs. Ma Thi*, 5 LBR 78.

[6] *Maung Ba Han vs. Maung Tun Yin*, 12 Ran. 629.

of the adoption as a relevant issue as, if adoption is proved, the adopted daughter would exclude the sister in the inheritance.[1] The findings of facts in an application for letters of administration will constitute a bar to a subsequent declaratory suit.[2] In granting letters of administration it is left to the Court to grant the letters to any person who would be entitled to a share in the estate, however small it may be.[3] One spouse cannot apply for administration during the subsistence of the marriage, though the couple are tenants in common each with an alienable and attachable interest in the joint estate, for the estate of a Burmese Buddhist couple becomes partible only on divorce, and inheritable only on death. When, therefore, one spouse inherits property during the marriage, the other cannot maintain an administration suit for it by the simple expedient of adding the inheritor, without consent, as a party to the suit.[4]

A suit for letters of administration can be expensive in time and money. When the estate is not more than Kyats 5,000 in value and they lie within Burma, any person who claims an interest in the estate, e.g. the widow, may apply to the Administrator-General for a certificate giving title to the assets. This cheaper and quicker arrangement cannot be availed of by the creditors of the deceased, and it does not apply to Government savings and bonds and provident funds which are governed by the Provident Funds Act and Rules.[5]

5. THE RIGHTS OF CHILDREN

The preceding pages have touched on the rights of children in the property of the family, and this section is, to an extent, a recapitulation.

We have seen the Orasa, the child of the breast, with his or her special place in the family. The oldest son steps into the place of the father on the latter's death, the oldest daughter into that of her mother, and sharing the burdens of the family, this oldest son, when the father has passed from the scene, or the oldest daughter, when the mother is gone, becomes the Orasa with right to a fourth share of the estate. We have also seen that this right accrues from the competence of the

[1] *Aung Ma Khine vs. Mi Ohn Bon*, 9 LBR 163.
[2] *Ma Mya Sein vs. Maung Soe Myint*, 1948 BLR 591.
[3] *Maung Tin Aye vs. Maung Maung Hmin*, 1950 BLR 78 S. C.
[4] *Ma Htwe vs. Ma Tin U*, 1953 BLR 29 H. C.
[5] The Administrator-General's Act, s. 31 as amended by Act 3, of 1957.

oldest son or daughter at the time of the death, and not necessarily the actual sharing of the burdens, and that this institution, reminiscent of Hindu law and custom, is becoming – if it has not already become – obsolete.

Other children share equally when they inherit: sons and daughters, regardless of age. As we have seen, the Dhammathats seem to have preferred sons to daughters at times, the oldest to the youngest, daughters to sons at times, but all these gradations have been swept away and equality is the rule.

The rights of children ripen only when the surviving parent dies or remarries. If the mother dies first, the family property devolve on the father, and *vice versa*, and so long as one parent survives, the children's rights are contingent, and it is the parent who takes charge of the family and maintains the children. When the surviving parent remarries, the children receive half the estate to share equally among themselves – a *per capita* sharing, as it is called. If the children have received their share on, or before, the remarriage of their parent, they acquire no rights, normally, to the estate of the second marriage. If there has been no such division, the children of the previous marriage, *Atet* children, may come in with the children of the second marriage, the *Auk* children, to share the estate. Division in such cases is *per stirpes*, through the different sources. The Atet children may take the Payin of their father, for example, and the Auk children the Payin of their mother; the Atet children may take a third of the Lettetpwa, and the Auk children the remaining two-thirds.[1] In general that is how the division goes, varying in detail depending on circumstances.

Joint living is no longer strictly necessary to entitle the children to inherit. "Filial relationship" is a vague expression. The daughter of a separated couple who has not maintained filial relationship with her father, it has been decided, can have her share in his estate in the absence of any widow or other children.[2]

A Kilita child "begotten while in pursuit of amorous pleasure" may inherit in the absence of children or descendants. The inheritance by such a child is confined to the properties in the actual possession of his or her parent, and the rights of the Kilita child are considered to be superior to those of a casually adopted Apatitha child. Though strictly on principle, a Kilita child may exclude an Apatitha, when the claim is made by the child of a Kilita by the husband whom the husband

[1] *San Paw vs. Ma Yin*, BLT 207.
[2] *Ma Saw May vs. Maung Htu Tha*, AIR 1930 Ran. 161.

and the wife have brought up in their home, and contested by the Apatitha child of the wife on her death, then justice, equity and good conscience will favour an equal division of the wife's estate between the two claimants.[1] Similarly, when the child of a Kilita daughter and the daughter of an Apatitha son compete for inheritance in the estate of the deceased step-grandparent, both are allowed to share.[2] A Kilita child is not an illegitimate child, but only inferior to children born of parents who live openly together.[3]

Grand-children, we have noticed, may inherit whether they are in-time, e.g. born of a person who dies after his own father, or out-of-time, born of a person who predeceases his own father. They inherit by right of representation, on behalf of their parent, and they share the inheritance per capita, not per stirpes.[4] Natural children's Keittima adopted children, and Keittima adopted children's natural children are treated alike as natural grand children for inheritance.[5]

It is not unusual to read in the newspapers announcements made by parents that they have disinherited their son as a Swanutta or "dog son" because he has shown them gross disobedience, or offered them painful insult, such as by marrying a girl they do not approve. Parents may similarly profess to disown a daughter as Swanutta, though "dog daughter" is not a common expression. Manugye lays down that "children who are wont to disobey their parents, who are accustomed to abuse and strike them, shall have no share in their inheritance." Unfilial conduct must be of a grave nature, such as where "a son has conducted himself as an enemy," and isolated cases of disobedience do not deprive a child of his or her inheritance even though the parents may in anger fix the brand of "dog" to his or her name and proclaim the disinheritance. Commissions of small theft of the father's property during the five years preceding a suit for inheritance were considered insufficient to forfeit the guilty son of his inheritance.[6] In the case of sons or daughters who marry against their parents' will, all they need to do, generally, is produce babies, and the parents, the new grandparents, become sweet again. This happens in every land, a human element which is larger than law.

We have seen a few other ways in which children may lose their in-

[1] *Ma Khin Kyi vs. Ma Than Tin*, 1949 BLR 273 H. C.
[2] *Ma Khin Kyi vs. Ma Than Tin*, 1950 BLR 55 H. C.
[3] E Maung, *Burmese Buddhist Law*, pp. 194–5 and p. 225.
[4] *Maung Po Thu Daw vs. Maung Po Than*, 1 Ran. 316 F. B.
[5] *Maung Sein Shwe vs. Maung Sein Gyi*, 13 Ran, 69 P.C.
[6] *U Po vs. Maung E Maung*, 11 Ran. 39.

heritance. One is by adoption, when the adopted child joins another family, and severs ties with the natural parents, losing the right to inherit to their estate. But as we have seen, when the children are of age, their consent is needed before the severance of natural ties may be made, and in some circumstances they may return to the original family later on. Adoption may also be ended by mutual consent of the adoptive parents and the adopted child.[1] Another way in which the rights of inheritance may be determined is by the divorce of the parents when the children are taken to the two separate families that emerge from one, and some children may break filial relationship with one parent, and the rest with the other. Here again, as we have seen, the Supreme Court has ruled that the severance is not as final and irrevocable as it has been thought before.[2]

When a son enters the Buddhist priesthood with intention to dedicate his life to the order, he leaves the lay life behind, and loses the right to inherit. A brief sojourn in the order as a Dunlaba Rahan does not affect his rights on his return.[3] "The question whether, under the Burmese law, a woman becoming a nun renounces her property and dies a civil death arose in *Mi Min Din vs. Mi Hle*, and it was held that a nun does not occupy a position analogous to that of a monk. The Methila nuns especially undergo no ceremony of ordination as nuns, but are simply lay devotees corresponding to religious laymen. Consequently there is nothing in the Buddhist law to support the proposition that a woman loses her rights to the property held by her, by reason of her having joined the order of Methila nuns."[4]

[1] *Chan Eu Ghee vs. Mrs. Iris Maung Sein*, 1953 BLR 294 H. C.
[2] *U Aung Kywe vs. Maung Po Hla Win*, 1952 BLR 15 S. C.
[3] *Ma Nyunt Sein vs. Maung Chan Mya*, 11 LBR 134.
[4] S. Roy, *Customs and Customary Law in India*, p. 349, case cited is in 1905 UBR.

CHAPTER SEVEN

BUDDHISM AND THE STATE

1. TRADITION AND CHANGE

The customary law of the Burmese family, though permeated with Buddhist ethics, is not, as we have seen, religious law or ecclesiastical law, and from many mundane affairs both the religion and the Buddhist priesthood keep strictly aloof. The influence of Buddhist ethics is strong, however, not in family relations alone, but in the behaviours of society itself. Thus the farmer who does not respond with enthusiasm to proddings to grow two crops instead of one is not just being lazy, but he is being Buddhist in contentment, in his values, in his goal to grow enough to provide his family and himself in food and clothing and the basic needs and to have a little over to offer to the village monastery or contribute towards the annual Buddhist festival. The villagers who do not respond eagerly to suggestions that they raise fish or poultry for food, or for the market, are being Buddhist too, and they do not wish to raise lives, even lives of animals, to slaughter and make money by.

Yet, the Buddhist farmer has to eat, and he enjoys meat in his meals. Here, in a simple and basic way, comes the clash between ethics and the practical needs of daily life. The clash occurs on many planes of social life, between ethics and needs, between traditional customs and modern notions, between the old ways and the new methods, the old values and the new, between what is and what the rising expectations want it to be.

The constitution that was adopted in September, 1947, was a modern constitution, and the state that came into being on January 4, 1948, purported to be a modern democratic state. True, in the fixing of the day when independence was to be proclaimed, the astrologers were consulted by the makers of the modern state, and the date moved from the originally planned January 6 to the 4th. on their advice. True, on the advice of the astrologers the hour of independence was fixed at 4.20 in the grey morning, thus requiring anniversary celebrations to commence at that sleepy hour ever since. But the builders of the modern state were the "elite" who had read widely, if not too deeply, of modern liberal thoughts and ideas, of Marxism, socialism and the rest. They also called themselves revolutionaries who were ushering in a new age.

The revolutionary elite, the modern ideas of democracy, the British principles and practices in law and government – the delicate, sensitive conventions and understandings included – the astrologers, the traditional customs and notions, Buddhist ethics, all these made a strange blend.

When one party dominated parliament and controlled the executive, the constitution worked well enough, or nobody noticed if it did not work or worked badly. When, however, the party broke up ten years after independence was gained and the revolution was ended, and the revolutionaries parted in search of new causes and new slogans, the strangeness of the blend became apparent. British constitutional practices needed British instincts and responses to work; British conventions can draw life from British sense of values only. The British practices and conventions, it was found a little too late, do not work too well with Burmese instincts and responses, with Burmese sense of values. The split of the party in 1958, and the convulsions that followed, the caretaker role assigned to General Ne Win, his return of political power to U Nu in April, 1960, after national elections had given the latter an overwhelming majority, the ouster of U Nu and the assumption by General Ne Win and a Revolutionary Council of military officers in March, 1962, all these, in the broad view of history, would seem to be incidents and events in Burma's search for a system of law and government that suits her best. "I do not accept," U Nu had written in 1959 when he was out of office, "that in cases where democracy may appear to have failed to take root, the reason is that – as given by some – the people are not ready for it. This is just not true, for democracy is men's inherent right and there is no single person or community in the world that can be said to be ready for it. A principal cause is the failure to adapt the institutional forms of democracy to local conditions ...and the genius of the people..."[1]

U Nu, and the traditionalist leaders of the group who shared power with him, set much store on Buddhism as a purifier of character and the national life, and thought that good Buddhists made good democrats, and to strengthen and perpetuate democracy in the country the surest way to proceed was to strengthen the influence of Buddhism on the individual as well as the state. This view was either shared sincerely or acquiesced in tactfully by the younger leaders who were modernist, if not marxist. "I have implicit faith in Marxism," declared U

[1] *Saturday Review*, December 26, 1959, reproducing a speech delivered at the World Conference on Religion, Dallas, Texas, in the Fall of that year.

Ba Swe, the socialist leader, who led the opposition to U Nu after the party split, "but at the same time I boldly assert that I am a true Buddhist. In the beginning, I was a Buddhist only by tradition. The more I study Marxism, however, the more I feel convinced in Buddhism. Thus I have become a true disciple of Lord Buddha by conviction, and my faith in Buddhism has grown all the more... We accept Marxism as a guide to action in our revolutionary movement and in putting this theory of Marxism into practice we are not going to adopt any carbon copy of somebody else's methods. The Burmese Revolution goes by Burmese methods and principles."[1] To clear up "ideological confusion" within the party and "at various levels of the leadership" also, U Nu felt it necessary to analyse Marxism at length at a national convention of the party, and reject it as the party's ideology. Democratic socialism, defined simply and without dogma as a community of sharing in which human dignity is upheld, was set as the ultimate goal of the party and the state, and the party split which followed within a few months of the convention, and the various other upheavals do not seem to have changed the goal.[2]

While Marxism was rejected, it was thought that Buddhism could be given a larger role to play in the state. Its revival, it was thought, would arrest moral degeneration, make men good and democracy secure. The Great Buddhist Synod, an assembly of eminent monks and lay scholars, met for two years in Rangoon, from 1954, to recite the texts and scriptures, to purify, edit, and record them for the future; in the 2500 years of Buddhism, these great assemblies had met at different places and times with similar purpose, and they had marked renaissance as well as the acquiring of merit by convenors and participants. At the close of the Sixth Synod, on May 22, 1956, which also marked the 2500th. year of Buddhism, and was the Full Moon Day of Kason, a noble day, U Nu proclaimed that measures would be taken to establish Buddhism as the state religion of Burma. The announcement, he said later, was made with the full approval of the leaders of the party, then united, and in response to a long and deep-felt want among the lay people and the priesthood to give Buddhism the status of the state religion to make the country's independence more real and complete.[3]

At the time the constitution was being drafted, proposals were made

[1] Ba Swe, *The Burmese Revolution*, Rangoon, 1952, pp. 7–8.
[2] U Nu, *Towards a Socialist State*, Rangoon, 1958.
[3] Chamber of Deputies *Proceedings*, August 17, 1961.

to write it in that Buddhism was the state religion. Aung San, the young leader of the national movement, was a modernist and a "realist" as he called himself, and he thought that Burma should rise as a modern and secular state, and while the Buddhist priesthood would have a vital role to play as educators and social reformers they should not mix in politics, nor should politics exploit them.[1] The traditionalists could not prevail, and the need to win the support of the minority peoples – many of whom were animists, Christians, and non-Buddhists – weighed against them. Aung San was assassinated on July 19, 1947, a few weeks before the adoption of the constitution, and a compromise section was put into it giving recognition to the "special position of Buddhism as the faith professed by the great majority of the citizens of the Union," and also to "Islam, Christianity, Hinduism and Animism as some of the religions existing in the Union at the date of the coming into force of the Constitution."[2] The same provision makes a pledge against discrimination on grounds of religion, and abuse of religion for political purposes. Other constitutional provisions which define fundamental rights also emphasise the right of equality and to non-discrimination and the right to freedom of conscience and worship.

The compromise arrangement remained satisfactory, apparently, for many years, and religion did not become an issue in national life. The Ministry of Religious Affairs gave its support to the Buddhist priesthood, the promotion of Buddhist studies, and such, and also made generous contributions to Christian missions working in the country, towards the translation of the Koran into Burmese, for example, and other such worthwhile activities of the various religious groups. In 1954 a public controversy flared up over the question of religious education in schools. There was a demand from the Buddhist Sangha and lay circles that Buddhism should be taught in the state schools, and U Nu as Prime Minister, proposed that if Buddhism was taught, the Christian Bible and the Islamic Koran also should be taught, and the children should be permitted to choose, according to their own religious faiths, for the constitution provided that religious education shall not be compulsorily imposed. U Nu pointed out, in a broadcast talk, that all citizens, regardless of their religious faith, served the Union in the different departments, bore arms in its defence, and therefore had justifiable expectations to be given equal opportunity and treatment. "Don't haul into the sphere of the sasana (religion)

[1] *Aung San of Burma*, Nijhoff, 1962.
[2] Section 21. See also sections 13, 20 and 22.

those acts which cannot be avoided on a political basis," he appealed, "I earnestly appeal to you to view religion and politics separately."[1] The controversy raged for a while and then cooled down, the Government promising to appoint a commission to study the question, and the Commission – if one was appointed – taking the usual time to investigate and report.

Religion may not be abused, nor dragged into political frays, and the abuse of religion is a grave offence in parliamentary elections which, if proved, nullifies electoral victory and further exposes the candidate to the penalty of disqualification.[2] Religion, however, was very much an issue – though only a silent one – in the parliamentary elections of January and February, 1960, in which U Nu led his party with the slogan for "Democracy" and his contenders, U Ba Swe and U Kyaw Nyein, the socialists, contested with promises to build the modern state and the economy by socialist planning. U Nu was careful not to promise, during the campaign period, to make Buddhism the state religion, but his pledge of 1956, and of September, 1958, at a conference of his faction after the split of the party, were echoes which rang through the campaign, loud and clear and legal. Buddhist priests, who do not have the right to vote, were known, during the campaign, to have gone round from door to door in some villages, asking voters to give their votes to U Nu as an "alm" to them, the priests, gently hinting that if the request was denied, they might deem it appropriate to leave the village for some other. A village without a monastery is an empty, indeed terrible, thing, and villagers took the hint. Elderly voters, bent with age, some nearly blind, were known to enter polling booths and cast their votes into the box that had U Nu's portrait on it, and sit down and pay their respects to the preserver and promoter of Buddhism. It was a huge wave of sentiment and emotion, of tradition and custom, religion and faith, that rolled through the country in the biggest and freest election that had been held since independence, and swept U Nu to victory. Charges were made afterward that U Nu had abused religion for political purposes, and protests were filed with election tribunals, but never successfully sustained.

Two commissions were appointed in April, 1960, one of Buddhist priests, and one of laymen, to study and recommend on the establishment of Buddhism as the state religion. The commissions travelled

[1] Broadcast talk of September 25, 1954.

[2] Election offence listed as number 16 in the 1st. Schedule, Parliamentary Elections Act, read with s. 36.

and studied in the country for eight months, inviting suggestions from Buddhist and non-Buddhist groups, seeking comments from many sources on circulated questionnaire. Comments were invited to suggestions that Buddhist education be made available, perhaps compulsory, to Buddhist children in schools, that Buddhism be made an examination subject, that those who had passed the examinations be preferred – on the ground that their moral character must have improved in the course of their study – to candidates who had not, in recruitment to the public services, provided, of course, that other qualifications were equal. There were murmurs also that when Buddhism was made the state religion, certain important positions in the state, e.g. the Presidency, the Prime Ministership and other Ministerships, should go only to Buddhists. There were debates, protests, demonstrations, and there were those who wondered whether the issue needed to be opened at all, and whether it might not undermine national unity in the anxious times at home and abroad. "Should this measure bring a chain of undesirable consequences," warned Thakin Tha Khin, leader of the Opposition in Parliament, "the Burmese Buddhists, who are the majority and outnumber the other citizens in politics, administration, and other sectors of the national life, will become culprits in history... Let us learn from our own history. Look at what happened when the Crown Prince Kanaung's advice to King Mindon to build munition factories was rejected because the Buddhist Sangha told the King that it was evil to bear arms. We were annexed by the British, like a chicken plucked by its neck. Not only did Burma come under British rule, the Buddhist religion too became dimmed then."[1]

The constitutional amendment which was finally passed on August 26, 1961, was mild and unspectacular. As previously pledged, the guarantees against discrimination on grounds of religious faith, were kept intact, and no special preferences were made for Buddhists in the matter of employment or holding of office, high or low. "Buddhism being the religion professed by the great majority of the citizens of the Union shall be the State religion." declares the amendment replacing the compromise formula which was adopted in 1947, but the other religions are also recognized, and the Union Government shall render "financial aid amounting to a minimum equal to 0.50 percent of its annual current expenditure for matters connected with religions." The other provi-

[1] Chamber of Duputies, *Proceedings*, August 17, 1961; *The Nation*, Rangoon, August 18.

sions were concerned with the promotion of Buddhist studies, the preservation of the scriptures and texts, the repair and maintenance of ancient pagodas and temples, the provision of separate hospitals for the priesthood, the convention of the eminent Sangha every year to report to and seek advice from in matters connected with religion.[1] The State Religion Promotion Act which was passed in supplement to the constitutional amendment went into some details, such as the observation of Buddhist Sabbath days as public holidays on which alcoholic liquor must not be sold, provision of facilities in state schools and the universities for education in Buddhism, the opening of elementary schools at monasteries where accomodation and facilities were available, and the presiding priests were willing to accept Government rules and requirements for such schools, and the allocation on Sabbath days of broadcasting time on the state radio for religious sermons or lessons.[2] The Act, and the constitutional amendment did not introduce new measures, nor provide for what was not already being done by common consent. Perhaps the proclamation of Buddhism as the state religion met and fulfilled a great and deep moral need, one could not tell. U Nu himself, in moving the amendment in the Chamber of Deputies, replied to critics who said that religion and government must not mix. "If the Government can provide for the benefit of the people of the nation in the short span of life of this existence," he argued, "it should not only be able to provide for their well-being in the inestimably long future existences but should actually do so. Since it is the disposition of people to perform those acts which leaders of standing have performed, the Government will have to assume leadership in the promotion of religion and Sasana. Since Governments themselves are propagating the notion that religion is a drug and opium, all Governments which cherish and respect religion must assume leadership in religion to resist that notion."[3]

A separate constitutional amendment was introduced and passed, this time against protests from some associations of Buddhist Sangha and lay people, guaranteeing the right to freely practise and teach all religions, provided that "no minor in school shall be taught any religion other than the religion of his parents without the previous consent in writing of his parents or guardian," and imposing on the Government the duty to "protect the religions from all dangers

[1] The Constitution (Third Amendment) Act, 1961.

[2] The Third Amendment was passed into law on August 26, 1961 and the State Religion Promotion Act on September 26.

[3] Chamber of Deputies, *Proceedings*, August 17, 1961.

including insult and false representation, made by words, either spoken or written, or by other means."[1] Here again, it is difficult to see how the amendment was found to be necessary when there were adequate provisions in the constitution and the penal laws to safeguard the freedom of faith and worship, and to protect religions from insult and abuse.[2]

There was joy and the beating of gongs, chanting of prayers, and the saying of "Well Done" when Buddhism was made the state religion. Government officials took to becoming priests for brief sojourns, some sincerely, some showingly; religious meetings were frequent and fashionable; it was difficult to distinguish between devoutness and religiosity. Turning Sabbath Days into public holidays added to confusion, for the Buddhist Sabbath, rotating by the moon, falls on different days each week. Sabbath Days were dry days for the official class and the "elite", and blackmarkets in liquor began to boom. When U Nu achieved the establishment of Buddhism as the state religion, people and the priests called him the promoter of religion, of the same standing as the Kings. A few weeks later, when he firmly resisted pressures and had the constitution amended to protect the other religions, people and some priests called him a traitor, of the same standing as those who would betray the Buddha himself.

Time was too short to tell what deep and lasting effects, if any, the legal enactments would have had. The political situation in Burma was bad when the laws were passed; it worsened after. The minority groups were restive before, and they became clamorous and aggressive after. The economy, to improve which plans had been drafted but never energetically executed, declined still further. On his return to office in April, 1960, U Nu had bent his considerable energies and talents to "easing tensions" between the parties by eating together, consulting on major issues, working through committees and advisory bodies on which the elder statesmen and leaders of the opposition parties were represented. He had the parties agree on a charter of democratic practices, such as fair play and equal opportunity at elections – with the party in power refraining from the use of its privileged position – and he had special measures instituted for ensuring an independent civil service, and a respectable elections commission. He also moved the Government – which was he – to build homes or abodes for the Nats, the guardian spirits. He urged the people to build 60,000 sand pagodas in

[1] The Constitution (Fourth Amendment) Act, passed on September 25, 1961.
[2] See section 130–A of the Penal Code, and ss. 295–298.

their villages, their wards in cities, so that the "16,000 problems" which he said the country was facing, might be solved with blessing. Some of those were traditional methods, and perhaps suitable to Burmese society. Like the establishment of Buddhism, they too, perhaps, had their meaning and value. U Nu probably "wants to revive a faith in which Burma takes pride," *The Times* of London observed," and also to revert to the traditional Burmese pattern of the ruler as protector of the faith, thereby justifying the exercise of power by the guardianship of a faith one of whose tenets is the renunciation of power as the aim of man's fulfilment... It is by shifts as this, not easily understood except with a deep knowledge of Burmese society, that the future of Asian countries is being moulded, as much as by the more easily comprehensible but often exaggerated calculations of political commitment or economic balance sheets."[1]

It is for history to tell whether U Nu was right or wrong; perhaps he was neither, or, perhaps, he was a little of both. The Daung Setkya, a well-known astrologer in Mandalay, who in the latter part of 1960 had predicted a victory for John F. Kennedy in the American presidential elections, came out at the end of 1961, not many months after U Nu had won his fight for the state religion, that U Nu's party was breaking up soon, that the building of the 60,000 sand pagodas was a mistake and an omen, that U Nu's star was on the wane, and a third force would enter the scene and rescue the country from disintegration.[2]

U Nu's party, built on massive victory, broke up in two in February of 1961, and in the early hours of March 2, 1962, Army troops quietly took positions in Rangoon, and small units went round to take away U Nu, some of his ministers, and several leaders of the clamorous minority groups, to safe and friendly custody in military camps outside the city. General Ne Win, whom political power failed to tempt in 1949 when he was made Deputy Prime Minister by U Nu, in 1958–60 when Parliament elected him Prime Minister to head a caretaker government, a man of few words, of sincerity and ability, who hated politics and had always told the Army to hold the constitution as a guiding light and to stay out of party politics, was back. Parliament was dissolved, and the powers of state were vested, by decree, in General Ne Win as chairman of a Revolutionary Council; the chairman and a small cabinet of military officers also serve as the Government. The laws and the

[1] August 22, 1961.
[2] *The Guardian*, Rangoon, December 31, 1961.

courts, the public services, and the various organs of the state, as well as the "spirit of the constitution" have been preserved alive, and strengthened. Political parties continue to function, and a constitution which is more in harmony with Burma is promised. The aim, it has been announced, is to unite the country, and work for the people's welfare, wasting no time or resources on idle words or fancy plans.

Asked about the state religion at a press conference, Brigadier Aung Gyi, a ranking member of the Revolutionary Council, replied that one religion should not be "overemphasized at the expense of another," and there must be freedom of religion. Sabbath Days have ceased to be public holidays; religious sermons have lost their time on the radio which will now devote itself to education and entertainment, raising some funds for improvement from commercial broadcasting; the slaughter of cattle for food – banned before – is now permitted, and people are encouraged to raise poultry, fish and pigs for their needs and for the market. But the Army, modernist and practical, is reformist too, and is concerned with the building of national character, though its methods may be different. Thus, horse-racing, a great revenue-earner, a sport of which General Ne Win and many of his officers were fond, has been banned as tending to run government officials and others into debt. "Show me one man who has become rich by betting at the races," the General asked of the directors and stewards of the Rangoon Turf Club whom he invited to lunch. Beauty contests in which young ladies appear in swim suits before admiring, often hooting, people, including elders, have also been abolished.[1]

Thus tradition tries in Burma to march together with change. Some may say that the traditional forms, the ancient customs, and perhaps the religious ethics too must be swept aside to make way for the full forward march to the new frontiers of the modern state. Some may say that the traditions and the customs, the religious ethics, the old values, matter much more than material progress, that man does not live by bread alone, and that we must cling to the past, or at least the present in which the past is still potent, and resist the tides of change. Perhaps Burma will go on marching the middle way, which is the Buddhist way, harmonizing the old eternal values of human society with the rising expectations and the changing modes of modern life.

[1] *The Guardian*, March 8, 10, 16, 1962.

2. RELIGIOUS USAGE

The Burma Laws Act prescribes that religious usage and institutions shall be governed by customary law – Buddhist law when the usage and institutions are Buddhist, Mohammedan law when they are Mohammedan. It falls outside the scope of this study, however, to examine Buddhist religious usage and institutions particularly when they are so far removed from affairs of the family and society, from lay matters in general.

When a Burmese Buddhist becomes a priest or *rahan* with intention to renounce the world, certain ties with his lay life are severed, and figuratively – though not entirely correctly – he "dies a civil death." He becomes divested of all his property and relinquishes all title to the same. The Buddhist monkhood is a mendicant order, and the only properties which a monk can possess are articles falling within the "four Requisites or Resources – food, clothing, lodging and medicine. Paddy land may be gifted to a monk for his future requirements to satisfy the Four Requisites and a lay steward, called Kappiya, may hold the gifts on behalf of the monk. A monk is not capable of inheriting property from his lay relatives as his personal property."[1] A Kappiya, or a Po Thudaw, who serves the priests at the monastery, does not "die a civil death" or lose ownership of properties.[2] Similarly a Buddhist nun, or Methila, does not die a civil death, as we have noticed before.

The Burmese Kings, as protectors and patrons of Buddhism, appointed the *Thathanabaing*, or head of the priesthood. There was no hierarchy of the priesthood, however, no organized church, and there were many schools, and each monastery, presided over by a senior priest, was a distinct and independent community in itself. When the British annexed upper Burma they found that the "office, functions and jurisdiction of the Thathanabaing could not be ascertained with certainty. The Thathanabaings were appointed to prevent corruption of the Buddhist scriptures, and to purge the Order of undesirable characters. In course of time they claimed and were sometimes permitted to decide not only questions relating to dogma and discipline, but also disputes concerning civil matters that arose between members of the Order, as well as between such persons and laymen. In the Regulation establishing the civil Courts in Upper Burma the tribunals of the Thathanabaing are not mentioned, and no jurisdiction of any sort or

[1] *A. R. L. P. Firm vs. U Po Kyaing*, 1939 RLR 311 F. B.
[2] *Ma Saw Win vs. Maung Gyi*, 2 Ran. 328.

kind has been conferred upon the Thathanabaing by any authority in that behalf. The recognition of the Taunggwin Sayadaw as Thathanabaing by the Lieutenant-Governor under the Sanad of 1903 had no legal operation. The Thathanabaing's authority has prevailed only in Upper Burma; the Lower Burma Buddhists do not recognize his jurisdiction. There is no 'consensual' jurisdiction conferred upon him by the *bhikkus* themselves at their ordination. Neither the Thathanabaing nor the hierarchy set up by him are mentioned in the Vinaya, which comprises the 227 rules by which the Sangha are governed."[1] The institution of the Thathanabaing thus fell into disuse, and the civil courts assumed jurisdiction when civil disputes arose involving the priesthood, such as the validity of gifts to priests, or the ownership of a monastery. The Vinaya are referred to where necessary, but where laws have been enacted, such as the Transfer of Property Act, and the Registration Act, they too must be complied with in addition to, or in supercession of, the Vinaya and the customary laws.[2] The Courts, it has been held, are bound to administer justice according to law, canon or lay, and where a gift of a monastery is found invalid for want of a registered deed, it was held good as a gift to the religious order, or Sanghika property, though not as Poggalika gift or one for the personal use of a particular monk. On the death of the presiding monk it is the duty and the privilege of the Sangha to elect a successor and a monk does not become the successor automatically by virtue of age or seniority. But where a senior monk has been tacitly acknowledged by the monks of a Sanghika monastery he becomes the presiding monk with the powers of control and management. Where there is no such acknowledgement, the new presiding monk must be elected.[3]

Sanghika property belongs to the Order in general – living within the four quarters of the globe – while Aramika Sanghika property belongs to monks resident in a particular locality. Ganika Sanghika property belongs to priests of a particular sect or Gaing. The power of control over the Aramika Sanghika property vests in the presiding monk of the locality; that over Ganika Sanghika property vests in the presiding monk of the sect.[4] A Poggalika gift, given to a named priest for his personal use, may be transferred. He may transfer property of a religious nature to another priest, property of a non-religious nature

[1] *U Pyinnya Thiha vs. U Ottama*, 13 Ran. 648 F. B.

[2] *U Zawtipala vs. U Thadama*, 1941 Ran. 209; *U Kelartha vs. U Pannewa*, 1940 Ran. 372.

[3] *U Zagara vs. U Sandawbatha*, 1948 BLR 866.

[4] *U Zawtika vs. U Kalyana*, 14 Ran. 566.

to a layman, and the transfers must meet the requirements of enacted laws. When a priest casts off his yellow robes and returns to the lay life, he is divested of his interest in the Poggalika property, and cannot dispose of it anymore.[1] When a priest dies without disposing of his Poggalika property, it devolves on the Sangha in general, and becomes Sanghika. A priest is competent to contract.[2]

Buddhist priests, and members of other religious orders, do not have the right to vote or to offer themselves as candidates in parliamentary elections.[3] In 1946, when the Legislative Council debated the question of franchise in the new constitution, the opinion of the Buddhist priests was sought on whether they should have the vote or not. The elder eminent Sangha expressed the view that priests should keep aloof from mundane matters; that politics bred anger and ambition and the emotions from which priests should strive hard to be free; that, therefore, they should not have the vote in parliamentary and other elections. The Young Sangha Associations, however, thought that if the people should choose to give the Sangha the vote, it would not be for the Sangha to refuse it, for theirs was to serve humanity, and not merely to escape from worldly woes. The Council, after considering the two views, accepted that of the elder Sangha.[4]

The influence of the Sangha on the political and social life of Burma has, however, been strong, regardless of whether they vote or not. Buddhist priests have been an invisible but powerful force behind many parliamentary elections; priests like U Ottama and U Wisara dedicated themselves to the nationalist movement for freedom, and priests took part in the hunger marches of 1938, and fell under police fire in the demonstrations of that turbulent year. Nationalism seeks its outlets, when pent up in all its fury, where it can find them, and in Burma it has often found the outlets among the young Sangha, and the students.

The Vinaya, with its 227 rules, imposes stern discipline and an austere life on the Buddhist priesthood. The Sixth Great Buddhist Council, extracting from the mass of rules the essence of correct behaviour enjoins the priests to avoid: "commerce; handling or accepting gold and silver; presenting fruits and flowers and prescribing medicines; trangression of the six precepts, giving livelihood as reason; attendance at *zats*, puppet shows, *anyein* shows, cinemas, theatres, circuses,

[1] *Maung On Gain vs. U Pandika*, P. J. 614.
[2] *U Pyinnya vs. Maung Law*, 7 Ran. 677 F. B.
[3] Parliamentary Elections Act, ss. 11 and 27.
[4] Legislative Council, *Proceedings*, vol 1, No. 11, March 14, 1046, pp. 404–32.

football games, boxing tournaments and other such entertainments; attendance at horse-races, boat-races, cattle shows and gambling; crime; entry at improper hours into towns and villages; entry into improper places in towns and villages; all acts which are improper for monks except of *pariyatti* study and *patipatti* practice of the Teachings"; and to be "fully robed in entering the town or village, and to observe the remaining precepts with one's life."

Buddhism could come under an eclipse, U Nu warned, despite its status as the state religion, if "unrestrained monks" flouted the Vinaya and misbehaved with impunity under the shelter of the yellow robes. "Let the restrained monks, the duteous monks, take definite action with the power of the Dhamma against the unrestrained monks who do not observe the rules. The Government too, in its desire to promote the prosperity of the Sasana and in its desire to fulfil to the utmost Lord Buddha's wish, will 'with the power of authority' take action against these unrestrained monks... The people should also reject and not worship nor offer the four gifts to them... If they do not reject, but continue to worship, take refuge in, and offer gifts to these unrestrained monks, they will be watering a poison plant. These people will then be accomplices in the destruction of the Sasana."[1]

The Vinasaya Act, passed in 1949 and amended and improved from time to time, establishes a system of tribunals on which respected Sangha elected by their communities sit and settle disputes which arise among the priests or in connection with the Vinaya or religious property. The Supreme Court retains only its supervisory jurisdiction on the Vinasaya Courts or Tribunals to see that justice is properly administered.[2]

[1] Chamber of Deputies, *Proceedings*, August 17, 1961.

[2] Reports and comments on topics discussed in this chapter by western scholars may be found in: W. L. King, *New Forces in an Old Culture*, Fred von der Mehden, "Buddhism and Politics in Burma," in the *Antioch Review*, Summer, 1961; George O. Totten, "Buddhism and Socialism in Japan and Burma," in *Comparative Studies in Society and History*, vol. 2, no. 3, April, 1960; Richard Butwell, *Civilians and Soldiers in Burma*, Fred von der Mehden, "The Changing Pattern of Religion and Politics in Burma," and Manuel Sarkisyanz, "On the place of U Nu's Buddhist Socialism in Burma's History of Ideas," in *Studies on Asia*, Nebraska Press, 1961; J. V. Jensen, "Burma's Experiment in a State Religion," *The Commonweal*, December 15, 1961.

CHAPTER EIGHT

THE LEGAL PROFESSION

1. THE BENCH

There are those who say that good laws make good men, and we need only to make the laws good, and the good men will follow. There are those who say that laws are neither good nor bad in themselves, but it is the men who, by working them and living them, turn them good or bad. Those of the first school plead: let us make good laws, borrowing from here or there the best of everything, and the men will grow up to the laws. Those of the second school argue; let us raise good men, educate the young generations, prepare them for the good life, and the good laws will write themselves in course of time.

It is important for countries like Burma which have re-emerged into the family of nations to choose between the two schools of thought, if the choice must be made, or to try and combine the two schools in working harmony, and then to set their course to their goals. When the goals are not fixed and the course is not set, confusion ensues, and the role of law in society is lost even as other social values and processes are lost or confused.

Governments have changed in Burma; men have risen to hold the reins of power, then passed on. But the goals have been fairly firmly fixed: they are to build a democratic society in which human dignity is upheld, and the people make their contributions to society and receive their shares enjoying equal opportunity. There have been differences as to what should be done first, what weight should be given to which; ideological indigestion and "those westernized political terms" have confused thinking at times.[1] There have been clashes of personality and the usual human failings and foibles, but none of the changes that have happened in the brief flash of time since independence – by history's reckoning – have touched the basic thoughts or concerned the large goals. The vital need is, therefore, to set the course and strive

[1] "To some extent the colouring of left against moderate, pro-Chinese against pro-western, enter into these new rivalries," editorially commented *The Times*, London, on March 3, 1962, the day after General Ne Win assumed power in Burma, "as it did into the old, though it would be unwise to interpret Gen. Ne Win's action in those westernized political terms. The army has acted against the seizure of power by an unprincipled faction."

on, and in this striving men of law have their roles to play – if they should choose to discover them.

Gone, however, are the "golden days" for the lawyers. Before the Depression – even Burma, hidden away from the world in a remote corner, was hit – lawyers could live in style with and on a good land suit, and having been called to the English Bar was in itself a passport to office or fortune. Leadership in politics, when that field started to open, went to those barristers, and they enjoyed a near monopoly of the well-paid and influential political jobs. The great ambition of the young college student was, therefore, to become a barrister and reach out for the abundant rewards, or to get into the civil service through competitive examinations or patronage. Values were such then that a clerk in a government office was held in higher esteem than a teacher, and there was a joke that it was of advantage to be a friend of the police constable – the ideal thing was to get into the service and be near the wielders of power, the next best thing was to know someone who was in, however low his position might be. Lawyers could enter at the top, as Ministers, for example, and it was good to know them, to have a barrister in the family as a son or a son-in-law. The people learned to look on lawyers as talkers and seekers and politicians, and, at the most, legal technicians whose assistance they needed to get through the formalities of the law if they had the misfortune to collide with it.

Lawyers and Judges had a hand in the drafting of the Constitution in 1947, and the Judiciary and the Bar have been consistently recognized as an important guardian of the Constitution. Yet, neither the 'England-returned' barrister, nor the locally trained advocate, could retain the reins of leadership and power. New classes arose, new values appeared. The nationalization of land removed a lucrative source of work for the lawyer; the new era, it was said, was for the doers and the revolutionaries, and those lawyers who could only quote from books and play with words had no place of honour in the dynamic society.

Fortunately, the dynamism did not destroy the legal system and structure. The laws have been kept intact and the Courts have continued to function through troubled days when armed insurrections swept the country and overran large parts of it, leaving only Rangoon free, sometimes. The danger, however, lay within the walls and not outside where there was open warfare. The Government was impatient, on the one hand, with what looked to it like the slowness and cumbersomeness of the judicial process, and exuberant, on the other, with its own power drawn from its predominance in Parliament and exacted on plea of the emergency. There were clashes between the Supreme Court and the Executive; in Parliament, Ministers and Members occasionally said harsh words in criticism of the Court's judgements or reflecting on the integrity of named Judges.[1] The Supreme Court, however, continued to exercise its power of judicial review, and has liberally construed its power of supervisory jurisdiction over the lower Courts.[2] No mortal struggle developed, though heavy pressures were sometimes brought to bear on the Judges, and the threat of impeachment was held up in a few cases when the conflicts were sharp.[3]

Pressures there were, and temptations too. The revolutionaries who took the reins of power when Burma became free regarded learned lawyers – especially those who had been to England, and spoke English with an accent – with awed respect. When, therefore, special commissions of inquiry needed to be appointed, the Judges were preferred for chairmen; when the President of the Union was elected in 1952, it was the Chief Justice whom the young political leaders chose. Judges have been elected Vice-Chancellor of the University of Rangoon, appointed leaders of delegations to the United Nations, and, in special situations such as those that arose in 1949 and the caretaker period of 1958–60, invited into the Cabinet. The awed respect that the young political leaders had for the Judges could not last forever. As they matured, became more experienced in statecraft, and grew more confident, their values fell into more correct perspectives; the awed respect faded away, in many instances not to be replaced by a more natural and more enduring respect and friendship. Often, the very tasks that were assigned to the Judges, political in tones, brought down suspicion or anger on them in the end. Invitations into the Cabinet, elevations to the Presidency, special appointments extended to retired Judges, also do not seem to have done much good in upholding the independence of the Judiciary or the confidence of the people in it. "When a man becomes a practising barrister and is then raised to a High Court Judgeship, and can then become Home Member and aspire to be Governor of Burma, how can he be entirely free in his deliberations and decisions as a

[1] E. g. speech in the Chamber of Deputies (*Proceedings*, April 8, 1960) by Leader of the Opposition ,Thakin Tha Khin, in which he stressed the need to uphold the independence of the Judiciary and refrain from putting pressures on the Judges – citing an instance where, he said, such pressures were applied.

[2] *D. D. Grover vs. A. C. Koonda*, 1955 BLR 54 S. C.

[3] E. g. suggestion made in Parliament by an Opposition member that the Chief Justice of the Union should have been impeached for a judgement he had rendered on the matter of foreign investment, *The Guardian*, September 26, 1957.

Judge?" So asked U Chit Hlaing, a respected nationalist leader, and a barrister, at the Burma Round Table Conference in London in 1931. "He cannot be free when he is aspiring to the post of Minister, and possibly the Governorship. I think, therefore, a High Court Judge should never become a Minister or Governor of Burma under the new Constitution."[1]

The clashes between the Executive and the Judiciary did not develop into mortal combat in the formative years partly because the political leaders exercised restraint, and also because they were enamoured of the forms of democracy. Having proclaimed to the world – and world opinion was very important – that Burma was a democracy, the political leaders were resolved to preserve the visible forms of democracy. "Can our Courts freely decide, without considering the wishes of the Government, and considering only the demands of justice according to the law"? So U Nu asked the national convention of his party after it had suffered a split, and provided the answer. "Our Courts have always acted freely. Oftentimes, we have wrung our hands in despair because a person whom the Government wanted to imprison is set free by the Courts, and oftentimes the Government has appealed against the decision of the lower Courts only to have it confirmed by the Higher Courts. When we have followed the case right up to the highest Court of law, and find that the decision still goes against the desire of the Government, we can but fold our hands, and watch the person go free."[2] The political splits and upheavals have probably enhanced the standing of the Judiciary and opened an opportunity for it to establish its real place in society. Those politicians who were inclined to look on the Judiciary as an obstruction on the path to the promised land now find, as their own fortunes change, that they need the protection of the Judiciary as much as, if not more than, the common citizen does, and that the independence of the Judiciary is not merely a desirable window-dressing but a vital necessity.

The organization of the Judiciary has remained basically unchanged. The judicial service, established at the turn of the 20th. century on the principle of separation of the Judiciary from the Executive, is still young and small. It is a permanent service which takes recruits from young law graduates – if they come forward – and from "insiders" such as court clerks, junior magistrates and judges. The young recruits go through periods of training and probation, then try cases and exer-

[1] Burma Round Table Conference, *Proceedings*, Rangoon, 1932, p. 310.
[2] *Towards a Socialist State.*

cise increasing powers, as they ascend the ladder of seniority and promotion. For many of them, the top of the ladder is a District and Sessions Judgeship exercising civil and criminal jurisdictions, both original and appellate, over a judicial district.[1] From that position, a man may move, by virtue of seniority and merits – and the good luck of a vacancy occurring at the right time – to the High Court where his appointment is secure, and independence of functions is guaranteed by the constitution. If he does not retire as a High Court Judge at the prescribed retirement age of 60, he may have an opportunity to become a Judge of the Supreme Court with security of tenure till he reaches the age of 65. The Chief Justiceship of the High Court ranks with a Judgeship of the Supreme Court in emoluments though it is lower in precedence. Judgeships at the district level, and of the High Court and the Supreme Court, are open to members of the Bar, and it has become customary, when vacancies arise, to share them out among practising lawyers and judges who are in the service.

The separation of the judicial and civil services still proceeds, and a recurring item on the agenda of the All Burma Bar Federation has been a demand for its completion, and a withdrawal of magisterial powers from administrative officers.[2] The day of the "civilian judges" – members of the Indian Civil Service, the Burma Civil Service and such who opt for judicial work mainly – is over. In the discussions on constitutional reforms for Burma, Burmese delegates to the London conferences had been more concerned about the Chief Justiceship of the High Court. "The Chief Justice should always be a barrister or advocate, and the quota of Indian Civil Service Judges should not be increased beyond one-third. In fact, we do look forward to the day when we shall be drawing on the legal profession for all Judges of the High Court..."[3] This proposal was adopted in the constitution when it was written in 1947, and the Chief Justices of the High Court and the Supreme Court come from the Bar directly, or from a senior judgeship after practice at the Bar. "Civilian Judges" have, however, rendered able service, and separation of the judicial and civil services would not

[1] There were 22 District and Sessions Judges before the War, and the number was reduced to 17 when British Government returned, and several judicial districts were grouped together. The pre-war strength in the Burma Judicial Service of 81 was increased to 104, and that in the Subordinate Judicial Service was also brought up from 87 to 124. *Report on the Administration of Civil Justice in Burma*, for the year 1946, published in Rangoon, 1951.

[2] *The Guardian*, December 31, 1960, reporting on the annual conference of the Bar Federation.

[3] Indian Constitutional Reform, *Joint Committee Records*, vol, 2. London, 1934.

have much useful meaning if its principal aim is only to exclude civilian officers from judicial appointments. "From the beginning of their service," a British High Court Judge, and later Lieutenant-Governor of Burma, had written, "civilians are constantly doing judicial work, always criminal, generally civil. In the five-and-twenty years or so that pass before they are likely to enter a High or Chief Court, those who have any aptitude or inclination for legal studies have had abundant experience and acquired a good stock of learning... It is thought by some not unintelligent persons that in the trial of civil and criminal causes it is an advantage for the Judge to have knowledge of the language, customs, and character of the people concerned. Apart from this, every High and Chief Court in India has civilian Judges, by common consent as well qualified as their barrister colleagues."[1]

The need for judges and magistrates to know the customs, cultures and character of the people whom they serve is as great today as before, if not greater. "There were grave misgivings," wrote a British barrister," when the first appointments of Burmese judges were made to the High Court in the early 'twenties. It was said that the age of graft and corruption was upon us. Taking them by and large these judges were an acquisition, some of them having high academic qualifications. They were certainly better than those of their brothers on the Bench who had been appointed in England with no knowledge of the country nor outstanding merits..."[2] The danger, however, lies in the fact that Burmese judges too, trained in the British concept of judicial aloofness, can lose touch with society.

Popular elements should enter more into the administration of justice. The jury system, suspended since the War, should revive, so that justice may come closer to the heart and the mind of society, and the laws may live.[3] An early suggestion made by the Administration Reorganization Committee also merits attention. "In the subordinate courts," it was proposed, "two district councillors or other local notabilities selected in much the same manner as jurors, should serve in rotation together with the stipendiary judge or magistrate as a bench for the disposal of appropriate cases, the decision following the voice of the majority. Such an arrangement would associate the public more

[1] Thirkell White, *A Civil Servant in Burma*, p. 281.

[2] Foucar, *I Lived in Burma*, p. 210.

[3] The editor of *The Guardian*, prosecuted for alleged breach of the Official Secrets Act, demanded a jury trial as was his right. The High Court granted his application, and the Supreme Court rejected the Government's appeal against the grant, saying that the lack of up-to-date rolls of jurors was no good ground for denial of a trial by jury. *The Guardian*, December 5, 1961.

closely with the administration of justice and tend to remove the impression, unfortunately too prevalent, that courts pay less attention to justice than to legal forms, devised originally for a different people in a different land, and better suited to commerce than to agriculture. It would also tend to remove suspicions of corruption in the lower Courts, as it is obviously easier and safer to bribe one man than three."[1]

2. THE BAR

Lawyers have fallen on lean times in the socialist state. The near monopoly that they had enjoyed on high political offices had been lost, and competition is keen now for the smaller political plums as well – and in any case the plums, these days, are likely to be more sour than sweet.

In the first sweep of changes lawyers looked rather like lost souls. At Bar association meetings their demands were for recognition of their status, as if that was something for the Government to grant, for "automatic promotion" from the lower grades of the profession to the higher by executive favour, for increase in fees for dock-briefs to keep up with the rising costs of living. After more than a decade of change and searching for stable values all round, lawyers too seem to be coming back now into their own, not by way of recognition of status or automatic promotions, but through a widening appreciation of their true role in society. Lawyers have been doing some active reappraisal of their role, and recent Bar Association meetings have seen a shift of emphasis from status to service, from promotions and dock-brief fees to legal aid, a strong Bar, high ethical standards, and improvement of legal education. Thus, for example, the All Burma Bar Federation called for provision of defence counsel for poor persons, the establishment of legal aid committees, and the reduction of stamp duties to reduce the costs of litigation and make justice less expensive and more accessible to the people.[2]

No distinction is made between "barristers" and "solicitors" in Burma, though practitioners are graded according to defined rights of audience. There are Pleaders, and Pleaders of the Higher Grade, with the right to practise in all civil and criminal courts subordinate to the High Court and all revenue offices subordinate to the Financial Com-

[1] *Report*, Rangoon, 1949, p. 23.
[2] *The Guardian*, December 31, 1960.

missioners. Pleaders needed special permission to appear in the higher hierarchy of those courts, while the Higher Grade Pleaders did not, but this distinction is now academic since all Pleaders, the last of whom were admitted under the rules of 1925 and 1928, have now moved up by virtue of seniority or through examinations, to the Higher Grade, or to be Advocates. The highest grade in the profession is that of the Advocate, and admission is open to those who have qualified at one of the Inns of Court in England, or to graduates in law of the University of Rangoon who, after a year's reading in chambers, have also practised as a Pleader of the Higher Grade. One may also enter and rise to the top grade in the profession through examinations conducted yearly by the Public Service Commission, which persons of prescribed educational qualifications and experience are eligible to take. The Ministry of Education offers courses to prepare candidates who intend to sit for the Pleadership or the Advocateship examinations, but the courses are not required, and candidates may prepare by private study. The rules of admission of Advocates and Pleaders are in need of reform, and several attempts have been made by the Bar Council, a statutory body which shares with the High Court the control and organization of the Bar, to revise them. There is, for example, need to expand and improve legal education in the country, to develop strong law schools in Rangoon, Mandalay, and other major cities, and to co-ordinate in legal education in general, at various levels. The rules also call for revision, to admit students who have qualified abroad in schools other than the Inns of Court – American law schools, Australian, or Canadian, where the systems of law are similar in the basic principles, and educational standards are high. Special privileges extended to those students who have been called to the English Bar – such as exemption from a year's practice as a Higher Grade Pleader before admission as an Advocate, and the calculation of seniority from the date of call in England – are small matters which pale into insignificance as years of practice go by, but they also may need to be revised to achieve standards of equality and to remove possible pinpricks and jealousies.

The great need of the Bar, however, is to find a role for itself in society. There is need for a strong and vigorous Bar as an important arm of a strong and independent Judiciary. Yet, noble motives alone cannot keep the lawyers marching. New incentives and new fulfilments need to be found in new roles. The public services have always absorbed large numbers of lawyers or young law graduates, and there have been proposals to appoint People's Advocates to assist and advise the village, town, and district councils when they begin to run the affairs of their small, self-contained and democratic social units. Legal aid may occupy members of the Bar usefully and profitably, and there have been proposals to establish a system of public defender service and even a People's Attorney General to appear, where necessary, against the Government's Attorney General in defence of the people's rights and civic liberties. Higher education is also a field into which lawyers with scholarly bents may enter to make their contributions and find fulfilling roles for themselves.

3. LEGAL EDUCATION

As there is need for lawyers to find new roles in society, so there is need for new directions in legal education to make new lawyers. The time seems to be ripe for reforms in legal education and in the organization of the Bar with which the subject is inseparably linked. A starting point must be the review of the aim and purpose of legal education itself. Obviously it is no longer enough to manufacture law graduates who will wander off with inadequate skills and, what is worse, only a vague sense of purpose. The law schools must inspire and stimulate their students who will disperse into the various important fields of nation-building activity; they should not stop short at being legal mechanics. Curricula therefore need revision and broadening; emphasis needs to shift. The law schools will also need to offer more variety, so that students may prepare for different kinds of legal career. In Burma, where resources are severely limited, it may be desirable that the law schools provide courses, even if only on an occasional *ad hoc* basis, for young administrators or diplomats. Practical training for young lawyers, in lieu of chamber reading, or to supplement it, may also need to come under the auspices of the law schools. The Post-Final training that is provided by the Inns of Court School of Law in London, and the special courses and seminars provided to meet such needs by the American schools in their summer programmes, and the Practising Lawyers Institute in New York, offer good models.[1]

There is greater awareness today that legal education needs to be improved and expanded. A period of growth seems ready to begin, and it is important that legal education grows up right when it starts

[1] Maung Maung, "Lawyers and Legal Education in Burma," *The International and Comparative Law Quarterly*, London, January, 1962.

growing again. The principal seat of legal learning has, so far, been the University of Rangoon in its law faculty. A graduate who has received his first degree in the arts or the sciences can work for two years, take the Part A and the Part B examinations, and earn the Bachelor of Laws (B. L.) degree which is not merely an academic degree but a professional qualification also. He can commence reading in chambers after he has passed either of the two examinations, and apply for enrolment as a Higher Grade Pleader on successful completion of the degree work. Classes are conveniently arranged in the mornings, from about seven to nine, to permit lecturers to go on to the courts or their chambers. The majority of the students also find the hours convenient to hold full-time salaried jobs or engage in business. Theoretically the classes are "full-time" for, before the war, there were two separate courses, the full-time taking two years to complete with three hours of lecturing every morning, and part-time courses running for three years with two hours of morning lectures. The merger of the two courses and their condensation into two years took place after the war, primarily to meet the great shortage both at the Bar and on the Bench.

Several proposals have been made for the improvement of legal education at the University. One was to introduce really full-time courses which would provide young students, arriving after their entrance examinations, with two years of preparation for legal study in the Intermediate of Laws, and three years of law, including procedure and philosophy, before they received their LL. B degree. They would then, after the usual year in chambers, enter the profession better equipped, it was thought, than the B. L. graduate who had only two years of part-time study and whose background might have been in disciplines which were not relevant to legal studies. The proposal was accepted by the University, and Intermediate of Laws classes were started in 1957 as an experiment, while the B. L. courses continued, their future to be determined on the results of the experiment. Shortage of teaching staff – successful lawyers are reluctant to take up full-time teaching – and changes at the University led to the suspension of the experiment in 1959, and students scattered into the various faculties to work for their first degrees before reading for the traditional B. L.[1]

[1] A good and thorough study on legal education, modestly called *A Brief Note*, by Hla Aung may be found in the Journal of the Burma Law Institute, Rangoon, Autumn, 1958.

Another proposal that has been discussed actively is the introduction of the Inns of Court system. The "Burma Inn of Court" which is proposed will be managed and controlled by the Masters of the Bench who are "three Judges of the Supreme Court including the Chief Justice, the Chief Justice of the High Court, the Attorney-General, ten members of the Inn elected by its members, who have practised as Advocates or Counsellors-at-law for at least ten years." Students would keep their terms, pass their examinations, and with a year in chambers behind them , be called to the Bar as Counsellors-at-Law. The fascination for the Inns system stems not only from the awareness of the need to improve and reorganize legal education, but from a desire on the part of the Bar to assume more direct control on admission and discipline and such "domestic affairs". The High Court, and not the Bar Council, has the control at present, and the Bar Council has the right to be consulted but not to rule.

The major task of nation-building in Burma, and other emerging countries, lies in education. There is a great hunger for it. The Government has been opening more schools each year, and tuition in the State schools is free and in the universities nominal. The target is to make primary education free and compulsory by 1970. There are now two universities instead of one, and "intermediate colleges" in several cities, one of which was inaugurated in the Shan State in June, 1961. Yet, the demand is for more. It is a healthy sign that the schools are full, and a most promising sign for the "Rule of Law" – which is a slogan as well as a rallying cry – that the law faculty of the University of Rangoon is drawing record numbers of students.[1] The Adult University in Rangoon, which prepares working students for external degrees, has started lectures for Part A and Part B of the B. L. examinations. Between the law faculty of the University of Rangoon and the Adult University classes there are over one thousand students every year, a good many of whom are senior officials of the Government, magistrates, and Members of Parliament. The University of Mandalay, at the insistent request of the Bar, which points out that the High Court sits in the city though legal education is available only in Rangoon, plans to organize its law faculty in the near future. The expansion is not solely to cope with the numbers, and basic changes

[2] Some 800 candidates offered themselves for examination in Part A of the B. L. degree in March, 1962, and some 200 for the Part B. The numbers, for the final examination, in the previous years were: 16 in 1946, and in the following years till 1958 – 19, 52, 74, 56, 59, 67, 68, 80, 98, 100, 115 and 158. ("The University of Rangoon," by Dr. Nyi Nyi, in the *New Burma* weekly magazine, August 16, 1958).

in the concept of legal education to meet the new needs are also being discussed.

Co-ordination and active and enlightened central direction are essential as reforms begin and facilities expand. They are all the more necessary because resources are limited, and should not be frittered away in scattered endeavours, or permitted to compete and cancel out one another. At present, the Ministry of Education, in whose administrative province all universities fall, conducts courses, whenever demands for them are felt, for candidates who are preparing for Public Service Commission examinations for Pleaders and Advocates. The Ministry of Judicial Affairs, the administrative machinery for the judicial services and the courts, has also felt the need to provide legal training of a specialised nature and refresher courses for judges, magistrates and law officers. Then, there are the universities which wish to expand or establish law faculties. All these proposals may perhaps be best directed and taken care of by a Council of Legal Education on which Judges, the Bar Council, educationists and the Government can work together, constantly surveying the general and deeper needs and applying available resources in the most intelligent ways to meet those needs. Under the general supervision and control of the Council, teaching and training institutions will grow, whether they are called Schools of Law or Inns of Court. They will develop their special strengths and share their resources where they should best be shared – in teaching, tapping the Bench and the Bar alike for part-time professors while relying on small but strong cores of full-time professors, and in library and other facilities. As the schools grow strong, they may launch teachers into the universities where the constitution and elements of the law can be introduced into the humanities curricula, or into the high schools where the need for such education has already become felt. The schools will also prepare research scholars to engage in the study of comparative law, or to record and analyse the laws and the customs of Burma – and we have seen, in this brief study, that though it is accepted that the laws and customs must march together, rising from the pages of the statute book or the treatises, to live and serve society, it is not always clear what the customs of the people are today, and how they blend with the laws that are being made by the legislative organs.

As the schools grow strong, Burma can better receive scholars from abroad, and begin to send scholars to exchange views, to enlarge the channels of knowledge, to compare notes and experiences – and basically, human problems are all the same everywhere – to participate in the greater sharing, and to give larger meaning to the "Rule of Law". Vast opportunities exist in the field of education in Burma, as in many new nations, and in legal education in particular the opportunities appear to be limitless.[1]

[1] Several good studies on legal education have been made in recent times, of which the following, among others, are useful: *Report of the Denning Committee on Legal Education for Students from Africa*, HMSO, 1961; report by Professor Julius Stone of Sydney at a seminar on the constitutions of the new nations, at Canberra, August, 1960; Report on Legal Education in India by Dean Carl Spaeth of the Stanford Law School to the Ford Foundation, March, 1960; a study on Higher Education, Law and the Teaching of Law, in British Africa, by Professor Max Rheinstein of the Chicago Law School, 1960; chapter on legal education by Professors Lasswell and McDougal in *Studies in World Public Order*, Myres S. McDougal & Associates, Yale University Press, 1960; John B. Howard, *International Legal Studies, Chicago Law Review*, Summer, 1959.

APPENDIX I

A LIST OF DHAMMATHATS *

	Abbreviated Name	*Full Name*	*Date of compilation*
1.	Mano	Manosara	...
2.	Manussika	Manussika	...
3.	Pyu	Pyumin	727 A.D.
4.	Vilasa	Dhammavilasa	1093
5.	Waru	Waru	1281
6.	Kungya	Dhammathat Kungya	1426
7.	Kaingza	Kaingza Shwe Myin	1629
8.	Yazathat	Mahayazathat	1629
9.	Myingun	Myingun	1650
10.	Dhammathatkyaw	Dhammathatkyaw	1733
11.	Dhamma	Dhammavinicchaya	1752
12.	Manugye	Manugye	1752
13.	Kandaw	Kandawpakeinnakalinga	1758
14.	Tejo	Shintezawtharashwemyin	1760
15.	Vannadhamma	Vannadhamma Shwemyin	1763
16.	Vannana	Manuvannana	1764
17.	Manuyin	Manuyin	1767
18.	Rasi	Vinnicchayarasi	1767
19.	Vinicchaya	Vinicchayapakasani	1771
20.	Manuvannana	Manuvanna	1772
21.	Pakasani	Vinicchayapakasani	1777
22.	Vicchedani	Mohavicchedani	1777
23.	Rajabala	Rajabala	1780
24.	Sonda	Sondamanu	1781
25.	Manu	Manu	1781
26.	Panam	Panam Pakinnaka	1781
27.	Rescript	Rescript	1784
28.	Kungyalinga	Vinicchayakungya	1803
29.	Dayajja	Dayajjadipani	1811
30.	Warulinga	Waru	1822
31.	Dhammasara	Dhammasararamanju	1845
32.	Amwebon	Amwebon	...
33.	Cittara	Manucittara	...
34.	Shinthapa	Shinthapa	...
35.	Kyetyo	Kyetyo	...
36.	Kyannet	Kyannet	...

* Extracted from *Kinwunmingyi Digest*, I., Mootham's *Burmese Buddhist Law*, and Chan Toon's *Principles of Buddhist Law*.

GLOSSARY

Apatitha	casually adopted child
Atet	above, or before, hence Attetpa property – property brought from a previous marriage
Auk	below, used, for example, to follow the downward flow of inheritance
Auratha	Orasa, child of the breast, usually the eldest, who is entitled to special share in the family property under certain circumstances
Deva	a divine being, an angel
Dunlaba Rahan	a man who becomes a monk or priest for a limited period
Jataka	stories of the earlier lives of the Buddha
Karma	the principle of causality in moral experience
Keittima	child adopted with intention that he become like a natural child and inherit
Kobo	price of the body
Pwe	variety show, dance, entertainment
Samsara	the round of rebirth
Sangha	the order of Buddhist monks, varyingly called the Pongyi, the Rahan, the Priesthood, the Bhikku
Sasana	the Buddhist religion
Shikoe	to bow down, kneeling and touching forehead to the ground, in respect to elders or superiors.
Shinbyu	head-shaving ceremony for initiation of Burmese boys as monks
Thathanabaing	head of the Order of Burmese Buddhist monks
Tripitaka	the three baskets of Buddhist scriptures
Theravada	also known as Hinayana, the "lesser vehicle," dominant in Ceylon, Burma, Thailand; the other major sect is Mahayana, "the greater vehicle."
U	"Mister" used before Burmese names; thus – U Nu; Maung and Ko are also "Mister" or "Master" of lower grades used to designate younger persons, or those of a lower status; "Nga" and "Mi" found before names in law report citations are lesser terms than "Maung" for males and "Ma" for females, and the use of these terms has been abolished in court; the ascending order for women is Ma and Daw, equivalent to Miss and Madame – "Daw" being used to designate a lady of status, not necessarily a married woman

APPENDIX III

BIBLIOGRAPHY

ARTICLES AND PAPERS

Thaung Blackmore, "Marriages in Modern Burma," *Eastern Horizon*, Hongkong, April 1961.

E Maung, "Insolvency Jurisdiction in Early Burmese Law," *JBRS*, December, 1951.

Furnivall, "The Fashioning of the Leviathan," *Journal of Burma Research Society* (JBRS), April, 1939.

– , "Manu in Burma," *JBRS*, August, 1940.

Alan Gledhill, *Burmese Law in the 19th. Century*.

– , translations of *Les Régimes Matrimoniaux du Sud-Est de l'Asie* by R. Lingat.

Hla Aung, "A Brief Note on Legal Education in Burma," *Journal of the Burma Law Institute*, Autumn, 1958.

– , "Sino-Burmese Marriages and Conflicts of Laws," same Journal.

Htin Aung, "Customary Law in Burma," chapter in Southeast *Asia in the Coming World*, ed. P. W. Thayer, Johns Hopkins Press, 1953, and in *Burma* anniversary number, 1953.

Maung Maung, "Lawyers and Legal Education in Burma," *International and Comparative Law Quarterly*, London, Jan. 1962.

– , "The Search for Constitutionalism in Burma," *Indian Yearbook of International Affairs*, Madras, 1960.

Mi Mi Khaing, "People of the Golden Land," *Atlantic Monthly* Burma issue, 1958.

Daw Mya Sein, "The Women of Burma," *Atlantic Monthly*, 1958.

H. E. Rance, "Burma Today," *Asian Survey*, London, July 1956.

H. Tinker, "A Short Survey of Burmese History," *The Guardian*, December, 1961.

Than Tun, "The Legal System in Burma, 1000–1300 A.D." *Journal of the Burma Law Institute*, June, 1959.

BOOKS AND TREATISES

Ba Han, *A Legal History of India and Burma*, Rangoon, 1952.

Ba U, *My Burma*, New York, 1959.

John F. Cady, *A History of Modern Burma*, Ithaca, 1958.

– , *Political Institutions of Old Burma*, Ithaca, 1954.

Chan Toon, *The Principles of Buddhist Law*, Rangoon, 1903.

Sir Charles Croswaite, *The Pacification of Burma*, London, 1912.

F. S. V. Donnison, *Public Administration in Burma*, London, 1953.

E Maung, *Burmese Buddhist Law*, Rangoon, 1937.

– , *Expansion of Burmese Buddhist Law*, Rangoon, 1951.

Sir Arthur Eggar, *Laws of India and Burma*, London, 1929.

H. Fielding Hall, *The Soul of a People*, London, 1904.

C. J. F. S. Forbes, *Burma and Its People*, London, 1878.

Forchhammer, *Sources and Development of Burmese Buddhist Law*, Jardine Prize Essay, Rangoon, 1885.
E. C. V. Foucar, *I Lived in Burma*, London, 1956.
Furnivall, *Colonial Policy and Practice*, New York, 1956.
J. Gray, *Ancient Proverbs and Maxims from Burmese Sources*, London, 1886.
D. G. E. Hall, *Burma*, London, 1950.
G. E. Harvey, *History of Burma*, London, 1925.
Htin Aung, *Burmese Juristic Tales*, London, 1962.
Sir John Jardine, *Notes on Buddhist Law*, Rangoon, 1882.
S. C. Lahiri, *Principles of Modern Burmese Buddhist Law*, Calcutta, 1939.
E. R. Leach, *Political Systems of Highland Burma*, Cambridge, 1954.
R. Lingat, *Les Régimes Matrimoniaux du Sud-Est de l'Asie*, translated by Professor Alan Gledhill.
Maung Maung, *Burma's Constitution*, Maritnus Nijhoff, 1961.
– , *A Trial in Burma*, Nijhoff, 1962.
– , *Aung San of Burma*, Nijhoff, 1962.
– , *Burma in the Family of Nations*, Amsterdam, 1956.
May Oung, *Leading Cases on Buddhist Law*, Rangoon, 1914.
Mi Mi Khaing, *The Burmese Family*, Calcutta, 1946.
Daw Mya Sein, *Administration of Burma*, Rangoon, 1938.
U Mya Sein, *Burmese Buddhist Law* (in Burmese), Mandalay, 1955.
O. H. Mootham, *Burmese Buddhist Law*, Oxford University Press, 1939.
U Nu, *Towards Peace and Democracy*, Rangoon, 1949.
– , *Towards a Socialist State*, Rangoon, 1958.
Lucian W. Pye, *Politics, Personality and Nation Building, Burma's Search for Identity*, Yale University Press, 1962.
D. Richardson, *Laws of Manu*, translation, Rangoon, 1896.
Sangermano, *The Burmese Empire*, introduction by Jardine, Rangoon, 1893.
Shwe Yoe (Sir George Scott), *The Burman, His Life and Notions*, London, 1910.
H. N. C. Stevenson, *The Central Chin Tribes*, Bombay, 1943.
Tha Gywe, *Treatise on Buddhist Law*, Mandalay, 1909.
Sir Herbert Thirkell White, *A Civil Servant in Burma*, London, 1913.
H. Tinker: *The Union of Burma*, London, 3rd. ed., 1962.
D. Woodman, *The Making of Burma*, London, 1962.

CODES AND MANUALS

The Burma Code, 13 vols., Rangoon, 1954, a collection of the statutes up to that year.
Burma Acts published separately as they are passed and in collection every year since 1955.
The Burma Courts Manual.
The Village Manual.
The Shan States Manual.
The Kachin Hills Manual.

REPORTS AND DIGESTS

Administration Reorganization Committee, First Interim Report, Rangoon, 1949.
Final Report, Rangoon, 1951.
Administration of Justice Reports, yearly, on civil justice and criminal justice.
On Juvenile Delinquency in Burma, Rangoon, 1928.

Parliamentary Proceedings, published for each day of sessions, in Burmese, separately for the Chamber of Deputies and the Chamber of Nationalities.
Legislative Council Proceedings, mostly in English till 1941.

Law Reports

Selected Judgements Lower Burma (SJ LB) 1872–92.
Printed Judgements Lower Burma (PJLB), 1893–1900.
Lower Burma Rulings (LBR), 1900–1922.
Upper Burma Rulings (UBR), 1892–1922.
Burma Law Reports, (BLR), 1895–1908.
Burma Law Times (BLT), 1907–1920.
Burma Law Journal (BLJ), 1921–27.
Indian Law Reports, Rangoon series (ILR Ran. or simply Ran.), 1923–1937 (from the establishment of the High Court at Rangoon to the separation of Burma from India).
All India Reporter, Rangoon section (AIR Ran.), a private reporting agency.
Rangoon Law Reports (RLR), 1937–47.
Burma Law Reports, 1948- with the Supreme Court section (S.C.) and the High Court (H. C.) section.
Full Bench is marked F. B.
Special Bench is marked S. B.
Privy Council decisions, before 1948, are marked P. C.

Digests

Kinwunmingyi Digest of Dhammathats, 2 vols.
Dunkley's Digest of Burma Rulings, 1872–1922 in vol. 1, and 1923–37 in vol. 2.
U Po Tha's Digest of Burma Rulings, 1937–55, published Rangoon, 1960.
Chan Toon's Leading Cases vol. 1, 1899, vol. 2, 1902.
Selections from the Records of the Hluttaw, Rangoon, 1889.

THESES

Khetarpal, S. P., *Marriage and Inheritance in Burmese Buddhist Law*, Ph. D., London University, 1959.
Khin Maung Win, *Some Philosophical Problems of Contemporary Burma*, Ph. D., Yale University, 1958.
Maung Maung Gyi, *An Analysis of the Social and Political Foundations of the Burmese Executive, 1948–56*, Ph. D., Yale University, 1958.
Maung Thein, *Customary Law of Burmese Marriage in British Burma*, Ph. D., London University, 1940.
Shwe Baw, *The Origin and Developments of Burmese Legal Literature*, Ph. D., London University, 1955.

OTHER PUBLICATIONS

Burma Gazette, weekly.
Burma Weekly, a bulletin of information published in English by Government Information, Rangoon.
Encyclopaedia Burmanica, in Burmese, on world and Burma affairs, published by the Burma Translation Society.
The Guardian, English language daily newspaper, and *The Guardian*, English language monthly magazine, Rangoon.
The Nation, English language daily newspaper, Rangoon.
Journal of the Burma Law Institute, Rangoon.

TABLE OF STATUTES AND CASES

STATUTES

CASES

A

C

M

N

P

Q

R

S

T

U

INDEX

GPSR Compliance

The European Union's (EU) General Product Safety Regulation (GPSR) is a set of rules that requires consumer products to be safe and our obligations to ensure this.

If you have any concerns about our products, you can contact us on ProductSafety@springernature.com

In case Publisher is established outside the EU, the EU authorized representative is:

Springer Nature Customer Service Center GmbH
Europaplatz 3
69115 Heidelberg, Germany

Batch number: 10830943

Printed by Printforce, the Netherlands